AF712824

Praise for *Keith's Book: A Love Story*

"The moment I finished reading *Keith's Book: A Love Story* by Linda Leonard, I realized it is really a work of art. A true picture of an incredible love story that should be widely read. Keith's Book is even a great educational opportunity to understand the basic archetype's of Jungian psychology. Intimate and masterfully written, congratulations to Linda Leonard on another beautiful book!"

—Arlene Landau, Ph.D., Jungian Analyst, author of *Tragic Beauty: The Dark Side of Venus Aphrodite and the Loss and Regeneration of Soul*

"*Keith's Book: A Love Story* tells the moving story of Linda Leonard's deep soulmate relationship—the dark as well as the light. I loved it! I had long hoped Leonard would write her autobiography, but this is even better. It's simultaneously playful and sublime. And it covers many of the important events of her life in a fanciful dialogue with her co-author, who impersonates some of the important characters in her story. Their story, including the life-changing impact of her writing on Bill's life, eventually finds its way into the dialogue. I found the book completely and utterly superb! Everything is just right—and nothing too much. I hope there's another book coming."

—Betty Cannon, Ph.D., Licensed Psychologist, President, Boulder Psychotherapy Institute, Founder, Applied Existential Psychotherapy (AEP), author of *Sartre and Psychoanalysis*

"WOW!! *Keith's Book: A Love Story*—I loved it. It's a brilliant episodic tale of personal adventures to Kilimanjaro, Siberia, Finland...and through the quest for love between Linda and Keith. I hope these wonderful short chapters are made into a TV streaming series so millions of people can see this brilliant work!"

—Susanne Short, senior Jungian analyst and founding member of the Jungian Psychoanalytic Association of New York, *graduate of the Jungian Institute Zurich,* publishes articles in the J*ungian Journal of Culture and Psyche*

"Our lives are composed of vignettes and emotions: pain, despair, madness, exhilaration, joy. Each moment becomes a catalyst for the evolution of the soul. In this memoir, fictionalized to disguise and protect, Bill Morris helps to ignite the memories and reflections of Jungian Analyst Linda Schierse Leonard, who, with her many books, has helped to guide us in the search for our Selves. In the end, we can see that Linda's life has been a grand, if tumultuous, Love Story. May we all find such exquisite love within the dark folds of the Mystery of Existence."

—Pamela Eakins, Ph.D., Sociologist, Counselor, and Educator; author of *Tarot of the Spirit*, *The Lightning Papers*, *Visionary Cosmology*, and *Priestess*, co-author (with Bill Morris) of *Conversations with Death*.

"*Keith's Book* is a love story through and through, with the ups and downs and the profound learning and joy that comes from caring and the sharing of two lives— growing with one another into a deeply trusting and soulful relationship even beyond death. It is beautifully written by Linda and her dear friend Bill who takes Keith's voice; one does not want to put it down. It was particularly touching to me, living in Aspen, home to Linda and Keith, where they experienced the gorgeous hikes and trails of the Rockies— a truly magical environment. I hear their voices ring out with laughter in the canyons, wishing they were still here."

—Nancy Swift Furlotti, Ph.D., Jungian Analyst and author of *The Dream and its Amplification; Eternal Echoes: Erich Neumann's Timeless Relevance to Consciousness, Creativity, and Evil;* and *The Splendor of the Maya: A Journey into the Shadows at the Dawn of Creation.*

"I want to thank Linda Leonard and Bill Morris for sharing *Keith's Book: A Love Story*, a masterpiece. What a splendid collaboration. I loved the playful/profound dialogue between Keith (masterfully channeled by co-author, Bill) and Linda Leonard in her deep memoir with her soulmate Dr Keith Chapman. What daring adventurers of the heart! There are two voyages: the achingly beautiful love story of Keith and Linda; and the deep, burgeoning friendship between writers Bill and Linda. They are all time-travelers, and I give thanks for taking me on this journey, and weaving together this timeless tapestry of tales and teachings, that deeply touched my soul."

—Hilary Cadwell, Ph.D., Psychologist; Dance/movement Therapist; Performance Artist; End-of-Life Practitioner

"This is a wildly unconventional love story that flourishes on the edge of the edge and sometimes over the edge. Two originals find and cherish one another, forging between them a third or fourth or fifth. Ultimately it is a story of redemption *a deux*, interspersed with great hikes and sacred adventures. This daring book reminds me what it was like to be a Jungian in a previous generation. *Keith's Book* is a wonder-filled book."

—Thomas Singer, MD, psychiatrist and a Jungian psychoanalyst and author of many books including *A Field Guide to American Cultural Complexes: The Battleground of the Splintered American Psyche*

"This book is the record of a decades-long conversation in which the title character, the partner of the best-selling Jungian author whose life he transformed, as she did his, is mostly silent, yet infinitely understanding and engaged. One can feel him hearing from the other side of their mortal lives about an individuation process he so truly shared that it made him whole as well as it continued through developing Alzheimer's to the conquest of his fear of death. Linda Schierse Leonard thrills at the chance her writing partner, Bill G. Morris, who voices Keith, has given her to continue speaking in dialogue with Keith, a psychiatrist who could listen with the same open heartedness with which she narrates all they discovered in the course of standing by each other through their individual recoveries from their tricky ways of avoiding life, even while seeming to live it to the full. Keith is with Linda through the facing and healing of formidable psychological wounds, and she is the one who helps the man who has shown so much compassion as a doctor to allow other professionals to care for him as a patient. But the real joy of this book is how broadly and deeply they travel through life together. Linda recalls how Keith gave her the courage to climb Kilimanjaro, look straight into the face of God in a dream even though it is part of a volcano, stare down a female celebrity who cannot stop serving up conversation during a classical concert, and share with her ever-curious companion the experience of having one's deadliest of sins interrogated by the cinema of Kieslowski. This book recognizes that individuation in later life is at its best when it is shared, and Linda does not disappoint the readership she has built since *The Wounded Woman*, of those of us like to feel we are her truest partner when she is telling stories on herself that only we can completely identify with. To read the book she has addressed so movingly to Keith opens a space in which any psychologically minded reader will feel much less alone."

—John Beebe, MD, Distinguished Fellow of the American Psychiatric Association and a past president of the C.G. Jung Institute of San Francisco, author of many books including *Psychiatric Treatment: Crisis, Clinic, and Consultation*

KEITH'S BOOK
A Love Story

By Linda Schierse Leonard, Ph.D.
with Bill G. Morris

CHIRON PUBLICATIONS • ASHEVILLE, NORTH CAROLINA

© 2026 by Chiron Publications. All rights reserved. No part of this publication may be reproduced, stored in a retrieval system, or transmitted, in any form by any means, electronic, mechanical, photocopying, recording, or otherwise, without the prior written permission of the publisher, Chiron Publications, P.O. Box 19690, Asheville, N.C. 28815-1690.

This work may not be used without permission for artificial intelligence training or development of machine learning language models.

www.ChironPublications.com

Interior and cover design by Danijela Mijailovic
Printed primarily in the United States of America.

ISBN 978-1-68503-680-5 paperback
ISBN 978-1-68503-681-2 hardcover
ISBN 978-1-68503-682-9 electronic
ISBN 978-1-68503-683-6 limited edition paperback
ISBN 978-1-68503-684-3 limited edition hardcover

Library of Congress Cataloging-in-Publication Data Pending

Keith's Book is a fictionalized memoir, based on the love story of Linda Schierse Leonard and her partner Dr. Keith Chapman, M.D. The characters, names, and events in this book are often taken from memories, enhanced by fiction, and depict a partnership and relationship from years ago. In some cases where actual names of people are shared, their specific actions are fictionalized and may or may not be accurate. In other cases resemblance to actual persons, living or dead, or actual events is purely coincidental.

Acknowledgments

From Linda: Bill, when you suggested we write a book together I had no idea it would break through a twenty-five year block. You offered me life and renewed purpose and meaning. I also learned more about different ways of writing and living. You are a master of metaphor, a brilliant writer, and so much fun with whom to write. I can't thank you enough for this gift.

From Bill: Linda, thanks for this journey. It was so fun writing it with you. With surprising synchronicities and miracles along the way. And thank you to my living miracles, Kristin, Cassian, Claire, and Syd, my family close and dear. Thanks also to Pamela Eakins, Ph.D., for her kind listening as therapist, co-author, and friend.

Contents

Foreword from Linda Schierse Leonard

A Word for Keith:

Sweetheart,

I just spread your ashes on the Stations of the Cross at the old Episcopal church nestled in the woods at Inverness. Remember that this church is where you had a spiritual conversion during the time when you were down and out and homeless. You worked there for room and board and kept the church and its grounds clean like your father did for your cabin during the Depression. Every flower had your name on it and spoke to me as I laid your ashes on them. The purple Irises, the golden Sunflowers, and the red Roses were especially grateful to be able to remember your love. And the towering redwoods drank in your ashes at their roots in a song that said "Hallelujah." Leonard Cohen was there singing in the forest grove behind the church.

But the most amazing thing happened the next day when I woke up. Your face was embedded between my breasts. I saw you smiling and felt your soul in my body and my vision. And I knew you were safe in me, in the earth of the church, and in your heavenly home. I wept and gave thanks and sang my own "Hallelujah."

PART 1

My Name is Keith

"To love is good, too: love being difficult. For one human being to love another: that is perhaps the most difficult of all our tasks, the ultimate, the last test and proof, the work for which all other work is but preparation."

—Rainer Maria Rilke

CHAPTER 1

Hello Again

Keith: Oh, you're here again, thanks for coming. I'm not sure why I'm still here. They say I live here now. But they're wrong. Everyday. I think I live somewhere with reindeer.
When I say that they just look at me funny.

I don't remember your name. My name is Keith. But I'm having trouble with recalling my last name. It rhymes with Captain. But then I'd be Captain Keith and that wouldn't be my last name, would it?

Captain Keith is kind of majestic, though. You know, Captain Keith. Someone that takes voyages here and far.

Why are you crying? I like it when you visit. What is your name again, sorry?
Please don't cry.

Linda: It's me, Keith. It's Linda. Your soulmate! We were with the reindeer together in Siberia.

Yes! You are a Captain—the captain of your destiny, of our voyage together.

But you are also Dr. Keith who is proud that he took the Hippocratic oath, proud that he helps heal the sick and wounded, proud that he can travel into the psyche of psychotic people so they feel understood, proud that when he worked as a family doctor in Colorado Springs that he let poor people pay him with a rock if they had no money. You told me they called you the "Rock Doctor." Now everyone calls you Dr. Keith, and even though you are a patient in skilled nursing at Balfour, you often diagnose the injured before the nurses can.

And I am proud to be your companion and love to see the sign on your door that says "Dr. Keith." I love to see the way you and JC, the Tibetan Buddhist orderly, relate and inspire each other if one of you feels down. I am crying because at 3p.m. each visit I have to leave and you don't know and can't know due to dementia that I can't stay longer. It is painful to leave you when I see the confusion in your eyes, when I know that this parting will happen over and over again until the day when you really can't know who I am. And I truly dread that time. But for now we are together on the ship you steer, sailing we know not where.

CHAPTER 2

Your Name Tag

Keith Chapman reading.

Keith: Good morning, Linda! I feel better today, clearer. Thank you for teaching me about me, about us. I like it. I also really like your name tag. It says:

Linda

You Love Me.

And I see it and know your name, and know that I love you. Isn't that a great way to start our morning? I think you're a genius. Your name tag that tells me I love you is superb.

Do people tell you you're a genius all the time? They should.

And I am Dr. Keith. Yes. Someone called me that today. Did you teach them that? The medical and room assistants call me Dr. Keith, and they're not being disrespectful, they're just familiar, gracious.

Linda, about that name tag. Is "You love me" your middle name or your last name? Ha, I love joking with you on clear days like this.

Can I tell you something that happened here last night? We had a new resident moving in, worried. He was a smallish man, and there was a little commotion down in his room. I went down the hall to see. I thought he was perchance bipolar, and I have a few tricks I used when bipolar patients arrived in my ER. So I went casually down to see if I could help. It felt funny. I didn't have a lab coat. Anyway, I asked one of the medical assistants what was up? The women assistants all looked unhappy, as if they were wearing skeleton masks.

I went in and had a few words with him. He was small, balding, with a rippling mouth. He was sitting far back on his bed, and each time a female nurse or assistant came in, he smiled and said, "I'm a super monkey lover!" and grinned.

On hearing that, the female nurse or assistant kind of froze, kept a couple extra steps distance from him.

I asked several questions, he never said "I'm a super monkey lover!" to me. I realized he wasn't bipolar. He was just terrified of women. And we can imagine the mother he had to induce that. And he used "I'm a super monkey lover!" like mosquito spray to keep women away.

So I went out and told the female workers the magic words to use. I told them to say, "I'm not your mother, and I'll never tell her anything."

And the female nurses and assistants started coming out of his room smiling.

They also started saying things like, "Thank you, Dr. Keith." It felt good.

So, Linda You Love Me, was I a crazy good doctor? Tell me if so.

Linda: Oh yes, you became a crazy good doctor.

Originally you wanted to be a coach for athletes. Immensely athletic, you won a college athletic scholarship out of high school. But after a year in college you joined the Navy—it was towards the end of the Second World War. You sailed to Okinawa. You were proud of being the ship's librarian; you loved and prized reading as a child and all of your life.

Dr. Keith Chapman with colleagues in Iran.

When you returned from the war, you found funding from the government to study and you chose to become a psychiatrist, though you also worked as a family doctor and in hospital ERs. You followed your inner self into psychiatry. You tried doing therapy with individuals but became bored even though you liked your patients. Then you started working with psychotics in hospitals. You travelled. You worked in Iran as a teacher and psychiatrist at a university in Isfahan and where you also worked as an ER doctor for Boeing. Your most intriguing story there concerned Anthony Quinn, who starred in *Zorba the Greek*. The actor was on a film shoot in Iran where he was thrown from a horse and sustained serious injuries, which you treated. It turned out that Quinn was afraid of horses which likely led to the accident. Your exuberance as you worked always reminded me of Zorba! I felt somehow it was no accident that you met him. You were forced to leave Iran quickly when the revolution overturned the Shah in the late seventies.

Stateside again, you started working with psychotics in hospitals. You had other adventures in the South, where you worked as a prison psychiatrist and tried to fight for care rights for the Black men who were not allowed to walk outside, while the white men could. The Ku Klux Klan got word of this and chased you in your car one night and also threatened your family (the second one) so you had to leave and returned to work at a hospital in Spokane. You had up and downs in your loves and family life. All before my time.

When I met you, you were working at Napa State, a large mental institution with its many wards and a pastoral campus.

There you were Dr. Keith, Captain of the Wards, in charge, exuberant leader, healing the harmed and mentally ill. This was later in your life, after your two families, and you took the post at the advice of your analyst who felt you needed a steady job at a late time in your life to have some retirement in old age. We met and set up life together in Mill Valley, then Sausalito. Our Mill Valley house was sparse, with no furniture, only a waterbed and mattress on the floor. I was happy to leave Bernal Heights in San Francisco where you protected me from a vicious stalker who followed me everywhere in The City.

Later, I convinced you to move to Boulder. You retired from Napa State, but started working "locum tenens" at jobs from all over the States to replace doctors on vacation. At one of these in Maine, you were ordered to discharge a patient whom you thought would just go out and repeat the same crime. You argued with a businessman director not to release the patient, but the director released him anyway. A few days later, three nuns were raped and killed in a church by this patient. Your work life always seemed filled with the harrowing.

But to me, Dear One, you were always a protector both as "mother" and "father" as well as love partner. As a man whose specialty was working with psychotics, you were uniquely fitted for me—a Jungian analyst and writer. On the one hand, you were very masculine as a former athlete but also extremely sensitive on the soul level. You had me deal with that stalker in court and also insisted I see the film *Misery* about a fan who takes a writer hostage, based on a Stephen King novel. And you challenged me to go on wilderness treks in Patagonia, to climb Mt. Kilimanjaro, and to look for wild elephants in Thailand. We did all that! You also encouraged me as I was writing my books and giving lectures. You weren't a writer so we didn't compete. But you worked, traveled, and lived out of your vivid imagination! And as a man of many moods and characters, you so appealed to me.

I think you are right that I'm a quiet pioneer and wild woman. My book on the Reindeer Woman is about this archetypal pattern and came from a dream that you had and which took us to Siberia, Lapland, and Alaska!

So, yes, Dr. Keith, you were a crazy good doctor, and perhaps a touch bipolar, in a fun way. I can say you were both.

CHAPTER 3

Linda, Where Are You?

Keith: I miss you. Where have you been?

Oh, we were dream travelers. Our hearts would whisper to us, tell us a story, a dream. And ecstatic, I would understand, my heart ignite. Oh, I heard the reindeer call, and had to go. Your heart would alight with my shared dream. And you said yes. Say yes with a laugh, sing yes, shout your brave yes of Love! And that's how we spent our lives, our money, our precious selves sharing of our inner journeys. Our dream journeys. We'd say yes and go. To live among the Even, the reindeer people in Siberia. To snowy Lapland, to the Arctic circle, to Alaska, we went!

I loved these adventures with you. You were so brave. Following dreams, living dreams, making our living for and from dreams. And you write them, I burn with them. Together.

And now as our fires burn less bright, I'm here. I love you for it, sharing dreams. Our thoughts, hungers, worries. We understood and reached for our visions. And now I wait for you here. I miss you.

Linda: Oh Sweetheart! I've been trying to reach you. I just had a terrible dream.

We were in Sicily and I decided to see a castle or monument. A big one, Romanesque style with rose pink stucco. I went in and other people were there. I looked around and decided to leave. But I couldn't find the exit door. I walked to some of the other rooms which led one to another. I wandered far but could see no door. By now I had walked a mile and just as I thought I had reached the exit I found myself in still another room. The place seemed deserted, but then I saw two women. They pointed to a door in the corner. But when I reached it, the door disappeared and I was alone.

By now the castle seemed to cover the island for miles. Suddenly I became very scared. Was I trapped in this huge empty place? Had I lost you? I thought of Kafka, and how he was trapped in "The Castle" and could never find the person in charge. The pink stucco walls became suffocating and the length of the rooms became longer. The shape of each room was strange and grotesque like a German expressionist painting. I began to realize I might never see you again. And then I woke up in terror.

Is this what you go through when you can't remember where you are? How horrible! How did we fall into this abyss?

Young Linda Schierse Leonard.

CHAPTER 4

Soulmates Meet

Keith: Oh Linda, good morning. I see you, I want you, I love you, Soulmate. How in heaven did I meet you?

Linda: Oh, let's talk. It's a good story.

I met you in 1982 on a trip to study Shamanism in Bali led by a Jungian analyst, Don Sandner, whom we each saw privately. Unknown to me, our analyst was describing me to you (who had two girlfriends at the time!) as a woman who wore ethnic clothes and looked like a Native American. I had written my first book but it wasn't yet published. The author copy arrived the day before I left for Bali and I took it on the trip. You were the first to read it in final form. One of your women was set to go with you on the trip but had a strange complication due to a surgery and couldn't come. You were actually trying to end this relationship with her since she smoked, gossiped and wasn't athletic.

On the first leg of the trip outside Sydney Australia's harbor, where we stopped a few days before reaching Bali, you were the last to arrive for the harbor visit. You were running and excited and in your hand were two magnificent roses—a white beauty that you gave to the trip's oldest woman, about seventy, and a glorious red romantic bloom which you gave to me. Everyone watched this scene in amazement, but with mixed feelings, since the only available man on the trip had chosen the woman he would herd, like a stallion does with his mares. I was delighted and pleased that you chose to honor the elder woman, too.

At the time of our meeting I was forty-four and you were fifty-eight. I had one marriage behind me and you had two with a total of five children. During the harbor tour, I planned to buy an opal jewel, my birth stone, as a wedding gift for the divine creator. You went with me and helped me pore over hundreds of opals until the right one shone forth. Today, forty-four years later, I still wear it in homage to the greater mystery as well as to the soulmate who helped me choose it.

After the harbor ride was over you asked me to have a drink with you. You ordered a beer and I chose a Coke. You asked me why I had chosen a Coke instead of a cocktail. I told you simply that I didn't drink. In surprise you said, "Women who don't drink fascinate me."

In Bali we stayed in a hut on the beach making love while coconuts were falling on the roof. We toured the island, went to the monkey temple where a clever monkey trickster stole away the glasses from a woman on the trip, and visited "The Balian": a shamaness who revealed secrets from our past and harbingers of the future.

As we returned from Bali to our stop back home in Sydney, suddenly I felt you distancing yourself from me. I couldn't understand and fell into a quiet despair until I realized you must have another girlfriend back in San Francisco. While leaving the plane, I saw a tall blonde woman about your age in the crowd eagerly awaiting arrivals. At once I knew that she was the rival from whom I needed to win away my new now unreliable Romantic Love.

I spoke of my travails with my analyst who, of course, also knew you very well. I told him I wanted a committed relationship with you, who was dating both me and another woman for several months. My analyst said with a wisened look in his eyes, "Don't use the word committed. Say instead that you want a 'sexually exclusive' relationship. I think that will work."

As it turned out the other woman did not want sexual exclusivity, but many partners to make up for the many years she spent as a Catholic mother of ten, and she had several boyfriends. But you, Keith, wanted your woman to be yours alone. And you didn't want to deal with her huge family of ten. And so, I soon had a steady vow from my soulmate.

Early on you challenged me to climb Mt. Kilimanjaro with you. I was amazed and in wonderment. You couldn't have known that this had been my secret wish as a child who was cooped up in an alcoholic home. To prepare we took long hikes and ran marathons—something I already loved to do. And so began our adventures together to be continued on a later day.

CHAPTER 5

Wading Through Pools of Worry

Keith: Yes, I was a confident, even bold physician. My work at the California Department of State Hospital-Napa was consuming. We provided care and services twenty-four hours a day, seven days a week for disturbed people, the captured, committed, evaluated, and whom we meant to save. I did so much talking, Linda, it was exhausting at times. And I had a mission, my pride, the Hippocratic Oath that I carried like a flag on a pole as I marched into crowded rooms of the truly sick and delusional. I felt for them, I felt, yes, somewhat a part of them. With them. What's better than a good delusion to make you feel great?

And I met all kinds and different flavors of sickness, some harmless, some life threatening. You have to stay alert. And I was alert. Sensitive to harm-doers. And I carried my oath To Do No Harm as my shield to walk among them, the injustices that they created or befell them. Linda, I saw so much misery.

And you, in serving and counseling your clients and lectures, you met them, too. One was delusional, followed you around as an aggressive, sadistic, controlling animal, a walking social disorder after your love. We talked about that, didn't we? And you became afraid of her. She shadowed you. You remember? I realized I had to do something to help you. I had to choose between my Hippocratic ideals, respecting a patient, and protecting you. And I chose you. I went after your stalker, went to drive her away. I set down my shield and meant to do harm. Do you remember? Because your love, your calm, your safe world was most important to me.

Linda, can you forgive me for that? Do you understand? I meant to chase your *de Clerabault's Syndrome* stalker away. I had to do it.

Oh, how and why did you ever meet her?

Linda: Keith, as you know, walking was always my greatest joy. I walked all over the streets of San Francisco—from top to bottom, from east to west. One day I was walking from my home in Bernal Heights, down through the Latin American Mission, over to Polk Street, and on to the place where my friend, Gloria and I planned to meet.

Suddenly, while walking, a woman rushed to my side. She said nothing but walked along with me. I recognized her. She had come to my lecture on "*Fathers and Daughters*," then later phoned to ask me for three consultations while her therapist was away. This was a frequent request from those suffering from the *father-daughter* wound so I agreed.

When I saw her in my waiting room, I could tell she was disturbed. But I kept to my promise and saw her the three times at my office on Clay Street. She presented her problem. She was lesbian but was attracted to straight women whom she thought were unconsciously gay. She gave a recent example.

A woman where she worked was standing in the parking lot by her car. Kali (as I shall call her) rushed over to proposition her, but the woman became scared and screamed to her to go away. I don't remember what I told her in my office but, I became afraid myself. Luckily I had my dog Heidi, a big black lab Doberman mix, with me. At the end of the last hour, Kali came toward me but Heidi came between us. Since Kali was afraid of dogs, she backed away and left.

Now she was here beside me. I asked her politely to leave. Kali said nothing but continued to walk by my side. Again I told her to leave. I asked her once more but with no results. And so began the saga of the Stalker. For an hour she stayed by my side. Nothing I said had stopped her. Finally, about an hour later, I reached the spot where Gloria was waiting. When Kali saw Gloria wave to me she turned around and left.

This pattern continued for months. I could go nowhere without Kali following me. I became more and more anxious. I called the police. The police chief told me he had no time to help. If I was a therapist I should be curing her and not bothering him. He did say, "We do know about her." And then he hung up the phone. At this time in 1980 there were no stalking laws —no way to appeal.

Gloria suggested I hire a lawyer. I found a good woman lawyer who told me the only way to end this harrowing experience was to find a witness to a physical attack by Kali. I could then file for a restraining order against her, although even that might not end her "following" attacks. The threat of following increased my anxiety; I began to drink again to relieve my fears.

I had met you, Dear One, and I didn't know you had tried to save me from her. You were secretly calling her to warn her and scare her off.

Keith: Linda, I did that. It was against my oath. To do no harm. But you living in fear in your home and neighborhood, I couldn't stand it. So I found her phone number. And I began to make calls, anonymous and harsh in the dark, to scare her in return. And…I was brutal. I had experience with the sick and manic. Knew the dangers and what it took to fiercely set boundaries. I did that. And didn't tell you. But it was ineffective. She was so severely fixated.

Linda: I'm glad I didn't know. But I do thank you. And perhaps you did have effect when she came once again to my home office.

I was talking with my long term client, a big man with a quiet voice, I heard a knock at my door. Hard knocking. So I excused myself. The knocking had to stop.

When I opened the door, there was Kali. Angry and cursing. I stepped back as she berated me. My client came to see what was happening. I went to close the door, put a barrier between us. But she stepped forward and pushed the door in on me. In an instant I was trapped behind the door against the wall, with Kali still pushing. My client came forward and gently moved her out and shut the door. I was blinking and breathing hard.

We called the police. Made a report. They didn't find Kali that day. But my lawyer was happy; we now had a physical incident… And a witness. She filed for a restraining order immediately.

Keith: I remember you wanted me at the trial. And I did attend. I sat in back to support you. I didn't want you to face her alone in the courtroom.

Linda: But Kali was seen, the judge understood instantly. A restraining order was put in place for years. With a hard warning of jail time.

Keith: For decades I hope. It seemed to help your fears a little, until you left Bernal Heights and you moved with me out of the city to Mill Valley.

Linda: Oh, that stalker continued to follow me for years. While in San Francisco I had to always be alert. And Keith, I was always glad I had you. You know that.

CHAPTER 6

In Music We Found Each Other

Keith: Ah, Linda, music enriched our soulmate relationship. Every summer we went to the Aspen Music Festival—ten weeks of bliss! We were silent but held hands, your little hand in my big one. We felt the music together. Our souls were united as though we were playing a duo.

Wagner was a favorite. But also the intricate Goldberg Variations. In ecstasy we listened to Beethoven, Mozart and Rachmaninov.

When Shostakovich created the threatening chords that disguised but signaled the horror of Soviet soldiers, we felt their impending doom.

Together we let Mahler's music lift us as one to birdsong and the divinity of Nature. We were one.

Aspen was exciting. We saw Itzhak Perelman on the street; we waved to him and he waved back. Later we saw him in New York at the premiere of a film about Beethoven. We also saw James Levine and Joshua Bell, James Conlin, and so many others.

I grew up listening to opera over the radio every Saturday. My family was poor from the depression but rich in culture.

You weren't exposed to classical music; your mother thought it was snobbish. But you told me your father said he liked Chopin. If drink hadn't taken control of his life, I can imagine the two of you being together like we are. I am a bit like your father because I am fourteen years older.

Linda: Yes, our love of music was like the great symphony of existence. Even when we were depressed, music could heal our wounds, infuse us with something greater. Remember when we wanted to go to Wagner's opera *Ring Cycle?* It was sold out when a man walked up to us with two tickets. The *Ring Cycle* became part of the book I was writing—*On the Way to the Wedding.* And the same happened when we went to *Swan Lake.* The ballet told the story of two lovers kept apart by the black swan, and we had to delve deep into the recesses of our own darkness so we could be free to truly love one another. Being a soulmate is not just about light and love. Diving into the shadows of human existence, both together and apart, leads to growth and strength to sustain and survive the vicissitudes of the finitude of human life.

I needed a partner who was courageous enough to accompany me on the difficult journey to heal the traumatic events of my childhood, and who could share with me the wounds of his own. Music helped us to enter the frightening abyss of humankind with every discordant note, to dare to open to the truth of the paradox that we are and to embrace the whole of our being. We are so lucky to have found each other—the pilgrim answering the call to walk such an arduous path to explore what it means to be human.

CHAPTER 7

Russia, Dostoyevsky, and Tears from Heaven

Keith: Here are my paintings of the golden domes in Russia. Do you remember that trip? So thrilling and perilous! We were lucky to go—and luckier that we came home alive! Looking back it was quite a dangerous time. But so exciting, an initiation of sorts.

Here are things I learned about you in Russia: you are a fearless traveler, you don't obey rules, and your angel's heart sings loudly at beauty you find. And that beauty was Dostoyevsky's Russia. You loved it.

Linda: Keith, how do you think about our first trip to Russia? It was with a group of psychiatrists to study the methods of treatment that were used in the Soviet Union. At the time I was actually writing about Dostoyevsky, my favorite author, for my book on addiction and creativity, and so I brought my notes along. At the border, they let everyone through but me and took my writing. They were poring over my Dostoyevsky notes to see if there was anything subversive. Dostoyevsky had opposed the Tzar, was Christian, and did not fit with communist rules. He may have been censored; I can't remember.

Finally, they gave my notes back and we alighted in Moscow—the city with Red Square and colorful onion dome cathedrals. Eleven churches are synthesized into a single magnificent architectural center.

We learned that the name "Red Square" is derived from the Russian word for "red" which means "beautiful" in old Russian. It was built in 1554-1560 to mark the defeat of the Tatars by Ivan the Terrible. And oh, the domes symbolize holy burning candles.

Red Square has been the historical site of many executions, riots, and parades, and speeches. It may have been the place where Dostoyevsky and others were brought to be executed for writing a journal that opposed the Tzar. Dostoyevsky was brought forward to be shot when at the last moment the Tzar curtailed the execution, and instead sentenced Dostoyevsky to years of prison in Siberia. He survived his imprisonment and later wrote an early novel, *The House of the Dead.*

Our group was given a tour of the Kremlin, a visit to Lenin's tomb, and to a thrilling performance by the all-male Red Chorus whose singing magnified the power of the Soviet government.

We were told to stay with the group and not go anywhere on our own. But I snuck out, to your chagrin, to visit Tolstoy's home in Moscow. I had no trouble going there and was glad I took the chance and went.

After a few days in Moscow, where we visited several hospitals using new methods of acupuncture and other unorthodox procedures at the time, we were told we had to leave early to visit Tashkent in Uzbekistan, the center of the historic Silk Road, a trade route for many cultures. Although we liked visiting Tashkent and were treated to an opera and a ballet, we were detained there for several more days, which would cut into our time in Leningrad, now restored to its original name of St. Petersburg. When we were finally allowed to go to St. Petersburg, we were given a hotel far from the city center and told not to go anywhere on our own. But St. Petersburg was the home of Dostoyevsky!

So we stole away and visited Dostoyevsky's home and the church where his mother had lifted him, after his birth, to the beautiful icon to be blessed by the Virgin Mary, an event that we thought protected him throughout his turbulent life.

Then we traced the steps of Raskolnikov, the protagonist of *Crime and Punishment*, to the myriad places he went in the novel. We went to the home of the Moneylender whom he killed thinking he was above the law, and to the hovel where he lived, then finally to the place where he met Sonya, the pure and gentle young woman who told him he could be forgiven if he confessed his guilt and, in repentance, bowed down to the ground on his knees and kissed the earth, watering it with his tears. Raskolnikov had been haunted by guilt and fits of madness and had a dream which showed his inner goodness.

By now we were far from the center of Moscow and didn't know where we were. So we hailed a cab and a man stopped in an ordinary car which we entered. We had been told that locals often drove to make some extra rubles, but not to take them, since many drivers were criminals. Since there were no cabs around we took it anyway. After fifteen minutes or so, you thought the driver was going out of town and we became suspicious. You told the driver to stop in a loud voice, but he paid no attention. Then you shouted in your most ferocious tone for him to stop and, scared, he stopped and let us out. We were in the middle of nowhere! Luckily another car stopped and took us to our hotel.

The next day was Sunday—Easter Sunday for Orthodox churches; they have a different calendar. We went to the Alexander Nevsky monastery and we were graced with incense and candles and the most mystical church service we had ever seen. The priests were many and in long flowing robes and massive beards and hair that matched their beards. Men were allowed to stand on the right, while women were to be on the left. The wonderful service was several hours long and afterwards we went to the cemetery since we were told that Dostoyevsky was buried there.

We saw the graves of Russian composers like Rachmaninov and other artists until finally we reached a huge cordoned-off area. There stood a huge gravestone with Dostoyevsky's image and covered by many bouquets of flowers. I burst into tears in thanks —tears sent from Heaven! You, Keith, were by my side and I knew we were as one. Perhaps this was our marital vow, unorthodox, but blessed by God—the God to whom Dostoyevsky also prayed as he had in *The Brothers Karamazov.*

The next day we were to fly back to America and we were ushered quickly through customs. Suddenly we were on the American stateside where we were swarmed, greeted, and told that a horrific event had occurred while we were in Russia. The Chernobyl nuclear disaster had irrupted on April 26, 1986, and it was the worst nuclear explosion in history. Hundreds of people were killed in the explosion, and thousands afterwards from the radiation exposure. The radioactive contaminated air spread north over St. Petersburg and on up through Scandinavia. Many animals were affected including the reindeer in the Arctic. It was forbidden to eat the meat of the animals that were killed due to exposure. Cases of cancer later multiplied due to the radioactive poison and continue to this day.

Once home, we could hardly take in this much news, much less how it affected us. Keith, your oldest daughter wouldn't let us visit her, fearful that we might have radiation in our bodies that could extend to her children!

To say how much our first trip to Russia affected us is beyond imagination. From the heavenly time at the Alexander Nevsky monastery, the Dostoyevsky soulmate pilgrimage, the ride in which the driver might have kidnapped and killed us, to the devastating news about Chernobyl and realizing where we might have been during that disaster—and yet, luckily we were saved and left to continue our soulmate mission.

CHAPTER 8

Kilimanjaro: Climbing High, Coming Back Low

Keith: Linda, do you remember when we climbed Mt. Kilimanjaro? We drank like fools and it nearly ended us. We went high, and came back low. It was a miracle that we, you and I, survived that. Do you remember that so crashing spiritual journey?

Linda: Yes, Keith. A few months after we met, you challenged me to climb Mount Kilimanjaro with you. You didn't know that this had been a major childhood wish, perhaps to compensate for being a child in a cage. I was impressed that you somehow discovered my dream of adventure. You told me I would have to hike up mountains with rocks in my backpack to get in shape. However I did not follow your advice.

On the day of departure, I could see you had been drinking. I think this is the only time I had witnessed this happen. I couldn't resist the temptation, so we both arrived in Africa a bit high. After checking into our hotel in Nairobi, I went outside to find you. I looked everywhere but no sign of Keith. Then I heard someone running and turned around. You were running towards me in your hiking shorts and mountain boots with a foolish smile that only you could have. You were a funny sight.

You told me that you had met some locals who had invited us to dance with them at their favorite nightclub. With a few drinks under my belt, I said yes, not thinking this might be dangerous. It was a place for Black folks in Nairobi. We were the only whites. We danced and drank all night, were wild, and had a blast. They drove us back to the hotel around four a.m.

Back at the hotel, we raided the minibar and drank all the liquor. It was almost time to leave for our first trek to climb Mt. Kenya at 17,057 feet. Not as high as Kilimanjaro, but in some ways a more difficult climb due to the incline, rocks and bogs. We were still drunk but we joined the group.

How we managed to do anything due to our inebriation is beyond me. The others were ahead of us, but the leader in charge stayed with us. We worked off a lot of alcohol in our system due to the exertion. Near the top were a bunch of boulders that seemed insurmountable. But the leader urged us to make the attempt. We made it. Once up we were to descend on another side of the mountain.

The way down was as hard, if not harder, than the ascent. The ground was a series of muddy bogs and we had to jump from one clump of grass to the next. This went on for several hours until we reached the campsite where the rest of the group had put up tents. Someone put up a tent for us and we didn't emerge until thirty-six hours later. Luckily the day after the climb had been set aside for leisure.

We left Nairobi and camped out in a beautiful place with baboons on the trees above us. One man left the site to pee, but when he looked up he saw a cobra staring at him. He backed away and hurried back to tell us his story. If the cobra was there, it could be anywhere—even at our campsite. Our good spirits were now tinged with realities of the place.

The next day, we left for Tanzania, where we were to climb Kilimanjaro from the backside, and not the way that locals named the "Tourist Trail." Our way involved starting out in a muddy jungle at about 7,000 feet. The top of Kilimanjaro was 19,341 ft. in height. Struggling up the muddy ground, climbing over tree limbs, and wondering if we would encounter animals on the prowl, we simply had to forge ahead. Finally, the first base camp appeared where we would spend the night. I was the last one to arrive and when I looked I couldn't see you. I didn't know how to put up my own tent by myself so the leader helped me. Still no sight of Keith. Eventually you came elated and said you had been the explorer Livingston making the jungle climb alone. I was very angry with you; you had abandoned me for your imaginary escapade. The leader was angry with you, too.

After waking up, we continued climbing. At one point we climbed something called the "Vertical Wall"—a formation that was difficult beyond belief. Local porters accompanied us to carry our supplies and the leader asked one to carry my backpack, because I was slow and he could see how hard the ascent was for me. You now stayed with us and were on your good behavior. One day it rained the entire time and we camped wet but glad that we were safe. We spent several days climbing until we reached 15,000 feet—the last site before the final ascent. On this day you ran ahead again. One man said, "He isn't pacing himself and will have a harder time on the last day to reach the top."

In the middle of the night, with flashlights fastened on our heads to see the rough ground, we started the final stretch. Soon we reached a section that was all scree—loose gravel rock that slid under our feet. It was two steps up, one slide back. You were now having trouble seeing. You were dizzy with a brutal headache. The leader appraised your situation and decided that you were suffering from altitude sickness and needed to be taken around the mountain and down to an elevation where you could breathe. I didn't know if I should go with you, but I also wanted to try to make the top. The leader convinced me to go onward. He told me he thought I could make it to the top. He had assigned two guides to accompany you around the mountain so you would be safe and get down to the camp where we would meet you later that day. Stopping due to altitude sickness was a frequent occurrence and had nothing to do with age. Many young people suffered from the same malady.

So up the scree, two steps forward, one step sliding back, I did make it to the point at 18,600 feet which was considered to be the top, where the successful reached their goal and were given a certificate of completion to prove we made the top of Kilimanjaro. I made it and was even ahead of two younger women in their thirties; I was forty-four at the time. There was an additional short stretch to a further higher point. The men went while the women, four of us, were happy to sit at the official climb post.

By this time we had daylight to see by. We had made most of the climb in the dark, so that we could make our way down to the campsite while it was light. Soon we joined the famous tourist trail. It was indeed by far much easier than our way up the back of the mountain. It even had huts at certain points along the way. It was like a regular hiking trail—no scree, no vertical wall, no impossible boulders.

When we reached the camp you were there. By now you had recovered and you were angry as hell at me for leaving you. I don't remember what I said or what the leader told you. But suddenly you started grinning and laughed. You told me you had had a dream that your internal goal was to climb the mountain. In the dream, round stones with strange signs on them went around the mountain as your path. You were to let go and accept getting to the top was not the most important now. Instead you were to follow the circular stones and slowly look at them because they contained ancient wisdom that you would need at this stage of your life. You understood that this was an archetypal dream—a dream you were meant to follow as your call to the Divine. You came and put your arms around me in a loving way. Somehow we had passed a test in our relationship—we had our individual paths, as well as our soulmate wedding path as One.

We reached bottom where everyone celebrated by drinking "banana beer." I drank too and was once again on a slide down to a drunken bottom.

You had to return to work in the States, but I stayed on in Africa. Now I was following the siren of alcohol. I went on a safari and met several Maasai men with whom I traded my broken watch for a snuff gourd with colorful beads. The Maasai used the tobacco to get a stimulating rush and for medicinal purposes to relieve pain, even heal wounds such as snake bites or other venomous stings. The Maasai were proud warriors known for their strength, courage and endurance. I enjoyed trading with them.

Then I went to Ethiopia still drinking and was finally told to leave the country which was at war up in the north. I went to London, still drinking. I went to an opera where a man picked me up and came back to where I was staying. The Indian men who ran the hotel kicked this man out and asked me why I was drinking so much. They wanted to help me. I was also supposed to meet my friend, Noni, to hike in Cornwall. I called Noni and she told me I needed to go home. Somehow I made the call to you, Keith. Maybe the Indian men helped me do this on their phone. You talked to me in a kind and loving voice and said simply: "Come home." Your voice was warm, but definite. Yes, I needed to come home to you and somehow to stop drinking. I made it to the plane and you picked me up and I was in your arms. Somehow I was able to stop drinking; I know you held me in your arms while I was shaking from withdrawal. I can still feel my desperation about the way drinking could take over my life.

So that's how our trip to the Kilimanjaro ended, with me in your arms.

CHAPTER 9

God Protects Fools, Drunks, and the Homeless

Keith: Linda, sometimes you meet despair, and it comes up and stares in your face. I remember I've done that. And it was hard.

I once had a psychotic patient in Napa. She was a slightly elderly woman, always laughing, smiling, a kind of ragged woman. They called her the Smiling Gypsy. And I'd sit at a table with her and talk to her. She was always so intelligent and kind, this Smiling Gypsy. On the edge of dementia, a little lost. And she always talked to me about cards, Tarot cards, she saw in her mind. It was her safe way of communicating, telling people about the secrets and the cards.

One day she told me that the Death card wasn't so bad. People feared it, but it just meant new things were coming.

But the worst card was the Tower. And everyone, even me, her doctor, drew it eventually.

She smiled at me, nodded and said, "When the Tower card comes to you, it shows a tower falling, two lovers falling from its top, all collapsing, crashing, crushing to the bottom. Dr. Keith, my dear one, it is the end of your world. Everything destroyed, your love, your worldly being, your family, home, your world. And the worst thing is, you must keeping living in it."

"Doctor, remember this when that card comes to you."

I took a breath as she looked me in the eye.

And the Smiling Gypsy told me, "When you draw that card, the Tower, you must say, 'Hello, it's you again. I guess I'll live with you for a little while. Let's take a walk. See if we can find our beautiful lost world. '"

And that became true, Linda. I had loves and families, and children, and I lost them all, didn't I? Oh Linda, what did I do? How did that happen???

Linda: Take care, Keith. I'll tell you what I know. You told me about your two wives and I'm not sure I have the whole story. You were very active with women and loved both wives, but both ended up angry with you.

I remember that both were "southern beauty queens" from wealthy families and their fathers didn't like you, since you did not come from riches.

I can't remember how you met your first wife; her name escapes me. But you were in medical school in Augusta, Georgia, and later did your internship and residency at LA General, and then Langley Porter in San Francisco. Then you lived in Terra Linda in a suburban area. And with her you had three children. You loved your children and took them into nature on adventures. The oldest loved going with you, but the two younger ones, a boy and a girl, began to hate you.

Unexpectedly, when you were forty, you began drinking and having affairs. You told me you went to Mexico, dated a wild woman, took a drug, and had hallucinations. The Aztecs were after you and you tried to escape on water skis pulled by a fast motorboat! You fell flat on your face in the ocean, but you were a top notch swimmer and survived. Looking back, it seems like you had a typical mid-life crisis. Your affairs increased and your marriage ended in divorce. Your wife was so hurt and angry that she never spoke with you again. I heard her voice on the phone the many times you called her trying to make amends; she was cold and mean and always hung up on you. The two younger children were so angry they cut you out of their lives. Your oldest daughter told me that her mother said she would never marry again because she could never meet another man as fascinating as you.

You moved to Berkeley and worked in the counseling program where you met your second wife who was studying there. Before that you went with many different women. One was a Danish ice skater and artist who left you in the end. Your second wife, Nancy, was also a suburban type woman. Two children were born from this union. During this period you worked out of state in Colorado and North Carolina, where you were chased by the Ku Klux Klan for lobbying for equal rights for the Black prisoners. They threatened your family so you had to leave and found a job at the state hospital in Spokane. There you lived once more in a suburban home and spent weekends by the lake going to parties with the neighbors. Your daughter Cathy said you were always bringing home strange chemistry sets and other toys and that you were a wonderful adventurous father. But Nancy grew tired of your adventurous spirit and had an affair with the next door neighbor, whom she later married.

Keith, you told me you were devastated by Nancy's affair which ended in your divorce. You were so depressed that you checked yourself into a hospital hoping to survive her treachery. After leaving the hospital, you wandered around aimlessly unable to work and became one of the homeless. You stood in line, ate from food at the Salvation Army, and made your way down to California. During this time you found women who would rescue you for a while, but these trysts ultimately left you alone and abandoned.

Then one day you met by chance or design an Episcopalian priest who offered you room and board in exchange for work cleaning up the church and its grounds. It was here that you had a spiritual conversion. In some ways you seemed to be repeating the life of St. Francis, who drank and lusted after women until he broke down asking God for mercy. This conversion was at the old wooden church in Point Reyes where you met your open heart again.

Finally you were able to find peace with yourself and felt solid enough to take on temporary work San Francisco as an ER doctor. You lived in a small cramped room above the Broadway tunnel by Chinatown. You met John Perry, a Jungian Analyst who opened an outpatient program for psychotics. When Perry was asked by an Iranian trainee at the San Francisco Jung Institute to come to Iran to work, he declined. But he told you it would be a good opportunity, so off to Iran you went. You loved it there for its beauty and peace and you didn't drink or date women, since that would break their Iranian moral rules. When the revolution against the Shah broke out, you had to leave quickly. You returned to San Francisco and went into Jungian analysis with Don Sandner, a doctor known for his wisdom, shamanic knowledge, and meditation practice. He told you to accept the psychiatric job at Napa State Hospital since you had no savings and needed to put aside funds for old age and retirement. Don was a grounding figure for you and he felt awe and admiration for your resilience and was intrigued by your archetypal dreams.

Always you had empathy for poor people and the homeless. But with your own experience as a "bagman," you became one of them. It was this sensitivity that made me love you.

So Keith, Dear One, your tower did fall. And with me, it rose again.

CHAPTER 10

Crossing the Lethe, River of Forgetting

Keith: Dear Heart, will you tell me again about Psyche's third task and the Tower. I love that story so much.

Linda: Yes. Psyche is one of your favorite heroines and her story is told in the tale of "Amor and Psyche."

Psyche was said to be the most beautiful girl on Earth. When Aphrodite got news of her, she became insanely jealous, because she was the Goddess of Beauty and Love and not to be outdone by a mere earthling. Aphrodite commanded Psyche's father to take his daughter to the top of a mountain and sacrifice her. But there the kind West Wind gently lifted Psyche and left her before the palace of Amor. When Amor saw Psyche he fell in love with the lovely maiden and during nights the two of them made love. But he warned Psyche she could never see his face during the light of day, and if she did she would lose him. A jealous sister planted suspicion in Psyche by saying her nightly lover was really a demon planning to kill her and urged Psyche to sneak a look at him.

Psyche succumbed to the temptation, saw Amor in the light, whereupon she was banished back to earth.

The jealous Aphrodite had a new plan to get rid of Psyche by giving her tasks no mortal could complete and thereby removing the ravishing maiden from her domain. Each task seemed insurmountable to Psyche, who would lament and sought to destroy herself. But just in time, a helper came to Psyche's aid so she could complete the task. The fourth task was to enter the Underworld and bring back a Beauty Box unopened. In despair Psyche climbed to the top of a Tower to throw herself off, but suddenly the Tower spoke to her. The Tower told Psyche she could enter the Underworld safely if she took a ferry and resisted pity for beggars by refusing them the coins that she needed to enter the Underworld. In addition, the Tower instructed Psyche not to give food to the ferocious dog that guarded the entrance to Hades and to keep it for herself. Psyche followed the Tower's advice, entered the Underworld, and brought the Beauty Box back to earth where she could give it to Amor.

In this tale the Tower helps Psyche to navigate the waters of the Underworld and travel the River of Forgetting which flows through Hades.

You, Sweetheart, have travelled the river of forgetfulness due to your Alzheimer's condition. So Psyche's journey through these dangerous waters is one that can bring you solace. And the Tower, now a beneficent image for remembering, has become your most valued ally.

And listen now, dear Keith. I too had a dream of Lethe, the river of forgetting and dream.

My dream: "I was on a small boat with a dozen other people. We entered a dark underground cavern and saw multitudes of angry reptiles chained to the cavern's walls. The crocodiles were especially ferocious and were snarling. But I felt sorry for the chained creatures and so did one other man. The Boatman said that we were there just to see this and soon would be out of the cavern."

Upon waking, I originally felt sorry for the chained reptiles and thought they should be freed. But a friend told me that they would eat us if freed. Later I realized that my sympathy for the captured beasts might be a warning to me about my codependency which was a dangerous addiction and a kind of forgetfulness. And now I think that was most probably correct. My codependency comes from my mother who rescued my alcoholic father. And I, too, was a codependent with you, Keith, till I learned to stand up to you, and became stronger. It made me a better person. And in some ways it allowed me to safely love you more.

Do you remember, Keith, we once slept in a hotel designed to resemble a crocodile when we visited the aboriginal sacred site of crocodiles located near Darwin, Australia? There were numerous live and dangerous crocodiles there as well as drawings of them on rocks. So you and I have been together in and among the crocodiles. You and I seemed to walk among danger as our routine. And I just had this thought: the crocodiles might relate to the dragons that St. George has to slay in the painting *St. George Slaying the Dragon*. Perhaps you have always been my St. George.

But, Keith, I'm strong, I don't need you to slay that dragon for me. And I don't need to feel sorry for those chained crocodiles. So Soulmate, how about it? Let's take you on a little stroll around the nursing home together. You can smile at me as I push your wheelchair.

Beloved Aspen mountain ridge.

CHAPTER 11

Hiking Electric Pass with the Famous

Keith: Once a well-known Jungian analyst and philosophical writer—I believe it was you, Linda—told me that in life you never know who you'll meet on the trail. But you better have fun while you hike it. And it turns out, on our walks, we found out famous people, bears, and deer all pee in the same bushes. You just need to be aware of who's standing next to you.

I loved our hikes in Colorado. I loved Aspen's beautiful sky, beautiful mountains, and fresh air so good you wanted to inflate you lungs and heart until they popped. Oh, we had fun hiking there together. And eventually I even taught you to duck when the lightning strikes. Remember Electric Pass? When you and I hiked it, the most important thing we learned was how to run.

Linda: Oh yes, Electric Pass! Our hikes in Aspen were always transcendent, but the one to Electric Pass above 13,000 feet was especially memorable; so much so that we wanted our ashes mixed together after death and strewn at the very top.

Electric Pass was so named because it was the spot that the dangerous lightning strikes hit first before hitting Aspen some 5,000 feet lower. The hike entailed climbing over loose rocks at the beginning, then a very steep slippery section before reaching a beautiful lake about two hours from the trailhead —the destination of most of the hikers. But for you and me, the next two hour stretch was the most beautiful climbing up through velvet green meadows adorned with brightly colored wild flowers—surely a gift from Heaven. At the very top was a small level place to sit before continuing to the very top, along a narrow ledge that gave me a touch of vertigo.

Intrepid mountaineer that you were, you encouraged me to traverse it. But we couldn't linger long because the lightning storms in the distance were oft destined to strike this sacred spot.

On one of these occasions we saw the lightning coming our way and heard the roar of thunder getting louder. So we started back, running down most of the way until we saw a familiar man sitting on a rock, winded, and seemingly smoking. Standing around him were several huge Black men waiting for him to catch his breath. Keith, you recognized him immediately and teased him saying, "If you smoke too much weed, you won't make it to the lake." The man looked up with his famous grin and laughed at the truth of your jest. Jack Nicholson acknowledged your assessment of his condition. We waved goodbye and continued down to the trailhead and then made our way to Aspen. The lightning had been terribly fierce in town and a great tree had been struck and was falling over. Back at our condo we cuddled in bed, pleased with the surprises of the day.

Another time, with our normal group of hikers, we attempted to climb alone up Maroon Bells pass and cross over and down to Crested Butte. The weather turned bad and we decided to turn around and let go of our hiking goal for the day. As we hiked down we reached the point where the West Maroon trail crossed the one to East Maroon Pass. There we saw a man riding horseback. He was accompanied by a number of large serious-looking, slightly scary men. Unlike his companions, the man on horseback was warm and friendly and waved to us as he rode by. In amazement we saw it was former President Jimmy Carter. We were thrilled and realized we didn't know the official way to address him. Meeting Jimmy Carter became the most important part of the day and overshadowed our loss of not reaching our original goal. This was surely a day to remember.

CHAPTER 12

Saul, Phyllis, and the Celebrity

Keith: We did bump into the rich and famous in Aspen. It's no lie that in Aspen they were there among our heavenly walks. They walked by on the sidewalks, on the trails, and we see them and they do not see us. And so, we walked on happy just being us. We went to concerts, film festivals, ski resorts… And had our fun. Oh, and we even loved the ballet. You remember? I do.

Linda: The ballet? Oh yes, I remember. One night at the ballet we were bothered by a man and woman sitting behind us; they were talking and dishonoring the great art they were there to see. You looked behind at them and recognized a celebrity. You were very angry at her self-importance but managed to control your anger. But I knew you were steaming with rage inside and I was hoping you could keep it from becoming an outburst that might cause us to be thrown out of the performance. During intermission the man sitting next to us stood up, turned around, and told the celebrity to stop talking during the dancing. You looked over at him in gratitude and admired the way he dealt with the famous person.

When the ballet ended, it started to rain outside. This man's wife asked us if we would give them a ride back; they had come by bus, leaving their car at their condo. Gladly we said yes and gave the couple a ride. On the way you asked them if they'd like to come with us for a coffee at Pour La France. We spent the time there talking and you told them about my book, *The Wounded Woman*. Phyllis, the wife, was a classical music singer who had studied at Juilliard. Saul, the man who had berated the celebrity, was a brilliant biochemist and formerly a pharmacist; he was very extroverted and fun.

Sometime later, although we hadn't seen them again, you recognized Saul walking by while we were eating lunch at the famous Hotel Jerome and you called out to him. He came over to our table and told us how Phyllis had read and liked my book and how much he loved hiking.

And so started a most wonderful friendship of forty years and for me the gaining of a great hiking partner. Saul and I took hundreds of hikes from which we returned elated. At first you were a little jealous because at your age, and due to your running marathons, your knees were compromised and you had several serious arthroscopic surgeries. But Saul and Phyllis became two of my closest friends and we attended lectures Phyllis gave on operas at the Aspen library.

Saul, who was not rich compared to most, focused on money and got up at six a.m. to check stocks. He was critical of your lack of concern for money and he was always nudging me to know what I needed to do around rich people. And he did criticize me for being unconcerned about money. Compared to most, Saul wasn't rich. But he hiked with rich people.

Saul and Phyllis lived in Florida and spent their summers in Aspen for the music festival. Phyllis didn't talk about money; she talked about her children, music, and singing students. She was very extroverted, upbeat and sweet. Saul and Phyllis were not intellectuals like you and me. Neither were their friends. They didn't know how to talk with you, who always wanted to talk about science—theoretically. Phyllis was able to relate to you because she was a "people person" and had a wonderful personality.

Phyllis and I confided in each other, helped each other understand our most important relationships. One summer your grandson, Josh, came to stay with us in Aspen. He was about twelve and his mother, your daughter Cathy, was hoping you could teach him discipline. You lent him your beloved bird book and told him to learn about these feathered friends.

Josh went to the "Ducky Derby" and came home without your book; he had lost it. You were irate.

The next day was Sunday when music lovers went to the Music Tent for the special concert with outstanding conductors like James Levine and soloists like Joshua Bell. You stayed home, but I went to sit on the first row. Soon I saw Josh come in to sit on the side of the first row, not with me but near me. Josh played the trumpet and loved music, too.

I had told Phyllis about the book incident with Josh and asked her if she could help me to know what to do. I had no experience with young children and was at a loss. Phyllis smiled and said why don't you ask Josh to go with you for dinner. A perfect answer but one that had eluded me.

I moved to a seat right next to Josh and when the concert was over I asked him if he'd like to go have dinner at a Mexican restaurant. He was so happy and said yes. At dinner I tried to draw him out in ways that Phyllis suggested. Then, with a big smile, he said "You're just like my Granny," referring to Keith's former wife. For me this was the greatest compliment. We walked home together and by the time we got back your mood was better.

Phyllis, Saul, and I began to hike up the backside of Aspen Mountain to its height of 11,000 feet several times each summer. Once we encountered a mountain lion but managed to back away. As a raving extrovert, Saul would engage every person we met on the hikes with a smile and a funny saying. His manner was so warm and friendly that he was irresistible. One of our favorite hikes was to start at the Upper Lost Man Lake trail, hike up to the pass at about 12,500 feet, and then climb further up on a steep rocky stretch to the top of the 13,000 foot ridge. From there we could look out over the vast view towards the direction of Leadville. On one of these hikes, lower down, we met the brilliant musician, Gil Shaham, the violinist.

Oh, you and I did touch the shadows of the rich Aspenites. Once, you and I were invited to an event in a rich man's house to raise money for the Aspen music school, and were the only non-rich people there. We did feel out of place. Gil Shaham was the musician invited to perform for these wealthy donors. After the performance, there was a dinner. You didn't like being with the wealthy and stayed sitting in your chair in the room where Gil Shaham played. Instead of joining the wealthy, Gil Shaham walked over and sat with you; I think Gil recognized another wise introvert and felt drawn to you.

This often happened to you. At the Telluride Film Festival, the filmmaker Werner Herzog came into a restaurant, saw you, and asked to join our table. I was there but they weren't inviting me; it was clearly your presence that drew them. Once there I could talk to Herzog, for example, because I had seen most of his films. Herzog is possibly the most famous and genius documentarians of our time. And there he was, a dinner guest to us. Life's surprising turns, and new friends among them.

Saul and Linda hike to the summit.

CHAPTER 13

Boiling in Jealousy

Keith: Linda, you talked of Saul just now. Saul. Saul. Saul. I feel… Angry. I know now I'm not everything you want. I'm older than you. My knees went, I couldn't do those pastoral hikes anymore, much less run down the mountain side away from lightning. So off you go without me. Hiking with Saul and Phyllis. Then hiking all the time with Saul, the happy laughing one! What? I feel truly abandoned by you.

When I grew up, we were so poor. I felt alone, different from the other kids, because I didn't have the clothes, the bike, the dog on a fancy leash, fancy things I longed for… To be with them. I was less, even in my family. They were poor inside, in spirit, didn't give me what I needed, alone in my room, alone in the woods, alone in school. I needed more. And so I made it, I made myself. I studied, I married, I had it all, clothes, houses, career. But I couldn't keep it… It was never enough. The rich "Sauls" would walk in. Laugh, be shiny, be superior. And then I lost to them. My neighbor took my wife. I lost my family, house, job, my very will to live. And then, I walked in misery.

I needed you! Needed you with me! I didn't need Saul in my life, any Saul. And you, you would just walk away, happy to explore those hills, mountains, pastures where the deer roamed and grazed free—where I couldn't go. I can't. Why do you leave me alone? I'm here, in this skilled nursing home for old folks. Why do you leave me?

Linda: Oh, Keith, Keith! We've talked of all this before. You know me. I'm right here in front of you. Don't disappear as you did into that angry canyon. I can't always run after you. You disappear. Hidden in your bushes of anger and slight. I can't always find you!

Yes, I had many hiking adventures with Saul, he and Phyllis showed up for me, I loved hiking. It's better not to go alone. So this came up again and again. Initially it was you who encouraged the relationship. But at a certain age you were unable to go on many of the hikes because you were, well too slow and your knees and feet hurt. We knew that. You knew that. You did become jealous, but I needed to be me, I didn't let that stop me from hiking with fast and ardent hikers.

I was poor like you. So I know how it feels. And I had to face it. Was I going to stay home, do nothing, or go by myself, or just hike on with others? Without you? And oh, Keith, sweet Keith, Soulmate… We did have to work out the jealousy through many fights and talks. We did have to remember our differences. We walked that path. And it was hard. Hard on you. Hard on me.

You were so jealous of most of my friends until you came to like them. One issue was our age difference; you are fourteen years older. Most of my friends made an extra effort to include you and draw you out, but you were an extreme introvert despite your times of expansion. You also had an inferiority complex due to growing up poor amidst your school friends who were wealthy. I knew what that meant. I knew it, too.

This burning coal of jealousy between us emerged especially in Aspen where we were the poor ones among the ultra rich.

I worked so hard with you about this issue of jealousy. I was also jealous when you spoke of other women. I wanted to be "special." When I felt jealous I would say so, but then withdraw. We became ghosts to each other. Hurting in silence. But you would always come to me making amends. I think what made our relationship work despite our differences, fights, and powerful independence, was the archetypal depth of our soulmate soulmate bond. You and I we were the same, at the point of trying to be someone, and we saw each other. We knew each other. And we needed. And we talked.

In some ways all this—this nursing home, my needing you, and you needing me, it becomes us seeing each other in a kind of memoir or on an opera stage, and what is important, right now, is my life with you, my being here now, right now. I'm here with you because you really understand me. And Soulmate, I do my best to keep you here, in me, in my memory and love.

Your jealousy was so extreme, and I admit I was jealous too. It was lightning that would strike. At any time. And I and you always worked on this to create tomorrow.

CHAPTER 14

Walking You to Beauty

Keith: Oh Linda, I need you. I'm upset today. I'm afraid and I don't know why. I feel worried, uneasy, I've got to escape.

This morning I had a dream: I had an important place to go, and I got up and I was naked. I went to my closet, and it was empty. I had to go to a party, but I had nothing to wear. I turned and there I was in the mirror, naked. And in the next room over, I heard loud laughing. I look again in the mirror and it's an old man's body but without a head. And I woke. I dressed myself fumbling like a madman. Oh, what's happening to me? Oh, I need you. Help me! I beg you.

Linda: Dear Keith, listen, I've seen this worry in you before. Seen how it takes you over. And then I and your floor nurse come to you, stand near. We know what to do. I loved this skilled nursing home with its caring nurses because it has art, wonderful art on the walls, in the hallways; it's an artful home. And I know you've loved art, and so the two of us walk you along the hallways, pointing out the art to you, stopping to look at each painting, the ones you love; I direct your attention to the ocean art filled with white sails and flying gulls, show you mountain peaks lifting up cupped snow like white wine toward sunsets, show you the laughing scenes of strangers eating happily in French cafes, and it distracts you from your fears. It works, you calm down. It's good medicine. I think that's a wonderful thing, using art and beauty to bring you back to yourself, back to being at home in a beautiful world. We both sought that, you and I, bringing in beauty to better our lives.

So rest now Keith, sit on this bed. Nap. I'm with you, be free to sleep.

CHAPTER 15

Keith's Good Demons

Keith: Once a patient on the ward wouldn't talk; she wouldn't utter a sound. I was making my rounds when the nurse drew my attention to her. She was a Black woman about fifty years old. I went up to her, looked her in the eyes, and said: "I have my demons too." She looked at me and laughed and said: "Dr. Chapman. You crazy." After that she began speaking like others.

Linda: Oh yes, Keith, that was you. And the instinctive way you cared for patients happened at Balfour, where you saw yourself as doctor of the ward. We were at lunch and a blind woman was at our table. She was upset because she felt that God was punishing her for actions in her past by making her blind. We tried to ease her anxiety and guilt and to help her be calm.

After lunch they showed a nature film and you made a point of sitting next to her. She could hear the dialogue in the film but couldn't see. You took her hand in your wonderful large hand, held it firmly with kindness, and described to her exactly the visual part of the film. With your care she was able to experience the film as though she could see.

Another time, a little boy about three wandered into the dining room and was crying. Balfour had parents bring their children in on certain days to relate to the patients. The boy was confused and lost; he couldn't find his parents. Everyone ached for his dilemma. Suddenly the little boy walked right over to you and touched your hand. You held his hand and the boy was comforted. The nurse told me this and said how wonderful that the boy felt your energy and came to you for love and care he needed.

Once, when we were in the common room, you heard a commotion down the hall. You wanted to go there to help the nurses because you felt responsible as the "doctor of the ward." A nurse assured you that they had things under control. Your devotion to healing was so strong that you wanted to be there to be sure the screaming patient was okay. But you were in your wheelchair and couldn't get there by yourself.

Whether it was demons or magic, I don't know, but as a doctor you had a gift.

CHAPTER 16

Horrors in the Haunted House

I left you later, went home. And as I sat, thinking about your worst bouts of panic and fear, and my own dread of them, my cell phone rang. It was a familiar number, and I answered.

"Hello, this is Dr. Linda Leonard."

"Hi, it's Dr. W., geriatric Doctor at Balfour. I'd like to hear your experience with Keith's delusions."

I took a breath. "Yes, Doctor, I have seen some things. He has had a number of tremendous bouts of panic. It's so frightening. It's very difficult. But I can tell you about five recent episodes."

* * *

Episode 1:

Keith (screaming): Linda, Linda. Get out! Get out! They are trying to kill us. You see these tubes hanging from my nose! They are trying to poison us by sending lethal gas through them. Get out! Linda, get out! Save yourself!

I knew the tubes were actually oxygen tubes so Keith could breathe better. In these extreme circumstances, art would not help him. I got out of his room and called the nurses, who came in and they were able to comfort him. JC, his Tibetan medical aide who liked Keith, was there to soothe him.

Doctor, I had witnessed many such frightening scenes before as a child when my father had DTs, the *delirium tremens*. My mother dealt with my father's crises and sometimes she called the police or EMS. Afterwards she comforted me in my fear and panic, and explained to me what was happening with my father, and that such attacks were due to alcohol. My mother was very good in this respect. She didn't make up false explanations. She told me the truth in a way that I could believe her. Of course, my grandmother was panicked and my mother, too. But as a child, I was able to keep a calm exterior, while no doubt suffering extreme anxiety behind my mother's outer armor of courage.

Doctor, these childhood experiences, on the one hand, set me up so I could understand what was going on with Keith, but also explained why I was so afraid of psychotics like my stalker.

Episode 2:

Keith (very frightened): Linda, Linda! Do you see that large yellow picture on the wall? Bring it here to me so I can see it better!

Linda: Keith, I don't see a picture on the wall.

Keith: Yes, it's there, the big yellow picture!

Linda (looking again): I can't see any picture.

Keith (more anxious, becoming horrified): Please, Linda, bring me the big yellow picture! It is broken. The big picture is broken!

He screamed this, repeating this in escalating horror. The world was ending.

The nursing staff came and somehow Keith was calmed. I remember standing in the room in shock.

Doctor, I later told my friend Arlene, a Jungian analyst, of this episode and she said, "That image of a 'broken picture' is from the end of the Bible and refers to the end of the world." And I then understood that Keith was seeing, the archetypal end of the world, and I thought to myself how we did indeed live in a broken world. His personal world was broken by Alzheimer's, but our human world was also broken by greed, hatred, and war. Keith's dream was both personal and archetypal!

Days later, the nursing home doctor wanted me to put Keith in hospice, but I refused. I knew Keith did not want to be left to die. The doctor was not too bright and maybe was herself scared by witnessing Keith's living nightmare of the Broken Picture. But I tried to explain to her that Keith was seeing the psychic reality of the state of the human condition. Luckily Keith's daughter and grandson had come from Spokane; I had called them. They understood the archetypal meaning of Keith's horrendous vision. And they agreed with me that to put Keith in hospice would be a grave mistake. By now Keith was relieved of his anxiety and said, "I want to live to be one hundred." So passed his vision of the end of the world.

Episode 3:

A phone call. Late at night I received a phone call from the Balfour nursing home. It was the night nurse, a man who had just been hired. Angrily and almost hysterically, he told me that Keith had just bitten him on the arm and he wanted to send Keith to the psych ward of a nearby hospital. The nurse assisting with him was a young, sweet Japanese girl who loved Keith and she had told the new nurse to call me.

I asked this bitten nurse to put Keith on the phone. Then I talked to Keith calmly and asked him to tell me what had happened. Keith told me that the male nurse was trying to kill him, so he bit the nurse on his arm in self-defense. The Japanese girl came on the phone and said that Keith had wounded his own arm and that the male nurse was trying to treat the wound. She handed Keith the phone again.

I said to Keith, "Sweetheart, you are a doctor. And if one of your patients was injured you would try to heal it."

Keith, now in a different state of mind, said, "Yes, of course."

I replied, "Well, that is what's happening now to you. Your arm was injured and they are trying to treat it."

Keith understood. Then the Japanese girl took the phone again and said while he was talking to me, he calmed down, and they were now treating his arm. I realized that if he talked to me, they could finish the treatment.

Once he was treated and calm, I deeply thanked her and she laughed warmly. I had seen her with Keith when I was visiting him and knew she was loving, kind, and compassionate. So it took a bright and lovely young woman, and not a male nurse, to end this episode well. When I came in the next day to see Keith, the male nurse was there and apologized, saying that he was new, and hadn't encountered Keith before, and put it down to "too much male testosterone between them."

Episode 4:

Doctor, I call this episode *The Robot*. Balfour nursing home took their patients on outings, and one day they took them to a museum in a nearby town. I had come early and was waiting for the van to return with them.

The first patient out of the van said to me: "Keith was afraid of a robot sculpture in the museum and he had to be taken out." This surprised me because, when I once asked Keith how he could work with psychotic patients, he said, "It is because I have no fear." This seemed to be true in my experiences of danger with him.

When he was wheeled out of the van, I asked him what happened with the robot. Keith shook his head and said, "Nothing. What robot?" I changed the subject and wondered if Keith indeed did not remember; he had Alzheimer's and recent memories were most commonly forgotten. Or, did he remember and was ashamed to tell me? I will never know; it would have been a mistake to pursue such incidents. No use to question further and risk another rupture. I let it go. I had learned this from the Balfour psychologist there.

Episode 5:

At one point Keith was put in a room with a patient suffering from Lewey Body dementia and other conditions. When I visited, Keith warned me to stay away from this man. Keith, the psychiatrist who was never frightened by his patients, looked at me in terror and said, "Do you see this man's angry eyes? He is dangerous! I need to have him removed from my room."

This situation was solved by the man's wife. She said her husband was kind and she requested that Keith be moved to another room. And so Keith finally was put in a room by the window where he could see birds flying and green leafy trees. He had another roommate, but one who was quiet and who mostly slept.

CHAPTER 17

Katherine's Explore Book Store

Keith: Do you remember the wonderful time we spent at Explore Booksellers—me reading and you writing? Explore was my home-away-from-home in Aspen.

The staff was literate and I asked David, at the desk, if he could recommend an author I didn't know. He suggested the Polish novelist, Henryk Sienkiewicz, and his trilogy, *With Fire and Sword*, *The Deluge*, and *Fire in the Steppe*. This last introduced us to *The Black Madonna of Częstochowa* and her role in protecting Poland from invasion by lifting her Holy Icon high above the approaching enemy; to this day, one can see the a scar on the Madonna's cheek due to the attack. And later you and I made a pilgrimage to honor the Black Madonna when we were in Poland.

Linda: Oh yes, we loved Explore and its owner Katherine! She was my best friend in Aspen, Katherine Thalberg! Daughter of Irving Thalberg, the man who originally made MGM—Metro-Goldwyn-Mayer Studios—famous and for whom the Irving Thalberg Award for Distinguished Filmmaking was given annually at the Oscars. Her mother was Norma Shearer, the silent screen star. Her father died when she was only one year old. She experienced her mother as cold and narcissistic. Katherine basically grew up alone, although she had an older brother, a philosopher, whom she loved. Her real family was comprised of all the books she read voraciously!

Katherine was an intellectual and had lived in Europe. As a teenager she went to a boarding school in the French part of Switzerland. Later she lived in Paris among writers and artists; she and I had culture in common. She didn't like the wealthy-society crowd in Aspen. She was very liberal, an animal lover and activist, and tried to get a law passed disbanding the sale of fur coats. The Society-Rich didn't like her and she didn't like them. She was married to the Mayor of Aspen, Bill Sterling, who lost an election after he supported her anti-fur campaign.

Katherine created Explore Bookstore and stocked every Nobel Prize winner's books, even if they didn't sell. The store was exquisite and in a historic Victorian building. Separate rooms for each type of book were part of the design: a special room for children's books where every Saturday a fairy tale or other favorites would be read, an entire room for literature, another for biography and writing, still another for history, philosophy and psychology. Upstairs was a common table for people to read and still another room for travel.

Katherine was a vegetarian and created a beautiful restaurant in a magnificent room with windows to look out at the mountains. An outdoor deck for meals during warm weather completed the restaurant's dining.

Keith, you were totally enamored of Katherine and admired her intelligence. She was extremely introverted. She told me she didn't like to be friends with writers, because when she met them in person, she found them disappointing and unlike their books which she admired!

How we came to be friends was quite a challenge and hinged on a synchronicity. One evening I was in the bookstore with a photographer, Charlie Abbot, who was taking my picture for a book cover and publicity events. We were upstairs in a quiet room next to Katherine's office. We heard a couple talking to her there. When the couple left her office, they saw me with all my books out on a table. The man saw them and said to me, "I love *On the Way to the Wedding*." His girlfriend said, "*Witness to the Fire* changed my life." I looked up and thanked them; they were dressed in warm ski jackets and I thought they were tourists in Aspen to ski. Before starting downstairs, the man said something as if to jog my memory, but I just smiled and bade them a good evening.

After they left the photographer laughed and said, "You don't know who that was, do you?" The man was Jane Fonda's ex-partner, Tom Hayden, the California politician. I knew that Jane Fonda had been reading my books to help prepare for her role with her father, Henry Fonda, in *On Golden Pond.* A participant from my workshop had been on a small plane from Santa Fe to Colorado, saw a man with the *Wedding* book, and asked why he was reading it. He was told it was to help Jane Fonda understand more about her character. Later he told me this story.

Katherine came out of her office and looked sternly at Charlie Abbot and somewhat surprised at me. (Actually we had a common friend, Phyllis Bronson, a dedicated biochemist, who wrote a book on mood and vitamins for women in pre-menopause. Bronson wanted Katherine and me to meet but Katherine was hesitant.) She said nothing just then but later, when Keith and I were in Explore, she approached us and said "I hope you are enjoying the books." I recall her treating us to dinner at her restaurant.

I'm not sure how things developed, but shortly thereafter Katherine and I met and our deep and stimulating friendship began. We had a lot in common: living in Europe, foreign films, reading the great authors, classical music at the tent, philosophy, intellectual life, disdain for the society social scene, and an intense passion to learn. Katherine invited you and me to her own Victorian home for dinner to meet Larry Krause, the famous physicist, and others whom she admired. Sadly Katherine died early at seventy from a vicious form of cancer. Her death marked one of the greatest losses in my life.

PART 2

Keith From the Mountaintop

"Believe in a love that is being stored up for you like an inheritance and have faith that in this love there is a strength and a blessing so large that you can travel as far as you wish without having to step outside it."

—Rainer Maria Rilke

A journey begins to find the sacred reindeer.
White Stag, book reproduction rights purchased from AI Art Shop 09/27/2025

CHAPTER 18

Independence Pass

Keith: Do you remember my telling you the dream of the Reindeer Woman? In the dream I was about to enter a reception at the Given Institute for psychiatrists—a weeklong seminar held every summer. I always felt an outsider there because the doctors have no experience of the collective unconscious—the realm from which archetypal dreams arise.

In the dream I don't want to go to the reception because it will be full of small talk and big personas. But I clench my teeth and go in. I was right. The atmosphere in the room is cold, heavy with false grandiosity. I see a white piano at the far end of the room and sit down to play. But I decide not to do that, because this is no place for Soul. I know I must leave. In another corner I see an exit, walk there, and go through the threshold. Suddenly I am in another space—a huge room with glass walls that open out into a forest. As I look around I see a mysterious woman run in. She is wearing deerskin clothing and her hair is long and tossed by the wind with twigs and leaves showing. In astonishment I ask, "Who are you?"

She answers, "I have just come back from running with the reindeer."

Now awake, I touch you and say "I have just had the most amazing dream."

You listened and said, "The Reindeer Woman must be an archetypal character for women. I was planning to write about women and animal spirits after I finish this book."

Linda: Keith, when we drove over Independence Pass (the narrow winding road with vertical drops and sharp corners that goes east from Aspen and climbs to 12,095 feet) you put on the radio. At the top of the pass, where the landscape looks like the Arctic, suddenly we heard Sibelius's symphony "Finlandia."

I looked around at the tundra and said, "Finlandia, the home of the reindeer; we need to go there to see the reindeer and the home of the Reindeer Woman in your dream." And so began our physical journeys to the Arctic to find actual reindeer. At the time, we did not know about the Sámi people who live there and follow the reindeer on their journey to give birth.

Independence Pass is a place where you and I hiked a lot. We even made love outdoors in some of the slightly lower hidden places. We also said after death we wanted our ashes mixed and spread over Independence Pass as well as Electric Pass.

CHAPTER 19

Cosmic Search for Reindeer

Linda: Keith, do you remember our first journey to find reindeer which showed up during your dream?

We started our trip in Paris at the International Congress of Jungian Analysts, whose attendees came from all over the world. In Paris we went to the Louvre, a Picasso museum, and the Eiffel tower. But the place we loved most was the gravesites of Sartre and Simone de Beauvoir. We sat for hours in the Luxemburg Garden where de Beauvoir wrote, breathing the atmosphere of her search for meaning.

After Paris we traveled to Hamburg where we visited my Danish hiking friend Peer Hultberg and his artist companion, Freddy. Peer, whose novels later won top prizes, took us to a special place for delicious varieties of herring which we have never forgotten.

From there we visited Kirsten Rasmussen in Denmark; she took us to the amazing museum, Louisiana, the repository of unique works of art. There is found "Gleaming Lights of the Souls" by Yayoi Kusama, one of the most beloved pieces in the museum collection. Then we went on to visit Stina Thyberg's Jungian friends in Stockholm, and finally boarded the train that would take us up to Lapland where we had heard the reindeer roamed.

The train was full with Swedish hikers; they got off for their trails aglow with autumn leaves.

Our stop was Kiruna; when we left the train we expected to see reindeer. We heard some locals chuckle. We hauled our baggage up a steep hill where we found a hotel with a glorious view. That night we slept soundly and years later you commented on how lovely it was to see my skin glisten in the dusk light of the moon.

The next morning we asked where the reindeer were and the twinkling eyes of the Swedish folk said: the reindeer travel. You must travel the land too to find them.

Before leaving Kiruna we learned about a shamanic group, the Sámi, who revere the reindeer. The Sámi are an indigenous tribe that live above the Arctic Circle in Sweden, Norway, Finland, and the Kola Peninsula in Russia. They revere the reindeer and follow them on their journey to give birth. Nomadic, they travel across the borders of these four countries with the reindeer as they move between the seasons.

So we went to the place where they gathered and learned that in the seventeenth and eighteenth centuries Swedish Christians had come to convert the Sámi people to Christianity, and many Sámi tribal drums were confiscated and destroyed by missionaries and officials. These actions were part of an effort to suppress Sámi shamanism and traditional practices. Their sacred drums were taken away and stored in a cathedral basement which later caught fire. The Sámi people were able to hide two of their drums and still use them to this day.

Upon meeting them, the Sámi folk were guarded; they had to save their traditions. We were stymied that we didn't know about them. Now we could see ourselves as "holy fools" on a mission to learn the mysteries of the Sámi and the reindeer they revered.

We rented a car and headed west, crossing into Norway until we reached Narvik. Then driving north, we reached the land of the North Pole, but still no reindeer to be found. We now knew the reality behind the chuckles of the Swedes who saw us as fools on our comic search for reindeer.

From the North Pole lands, and still no sight of the reindeer, we decided to head south. After an hour we entered an unusual mountainous canyon; the atmosphere felt mystical. Keith, you said, "Soon, I think we will see reindeer." And as usual you were right. A small group of reindeer were grazing. Among them was a stunning white reindeer. Later we learned that the White Reindeer are regarded by the Sámi people as mysterious reincarnations of people who have died. For this reason it is forbidden to kill them.

We spent time with these mystical beings in awe of their spiritual power.

Then we continued south to Kautokeino, a town where Sámi culture was preserved in a museum and in a library. We spoke to a man in charge of the library. We asked questions about their culture but, like many Sámi people, he was very guarded, and for good reason since the Sámi folk had been abused by Christians and other European groups. However, he led us to books in English in the library so that we could learn about his people.

An animistic, shamanistic, and polytheistic group, the Sámi believe spirits inhabit Nature and perform healing rituals. They use a sacred ceremonial drum made from reindeer hide that has symbols which represents different layers of the spiritual world and the reindeer and other creatures of Nature. The shamans use the drum to enter a trance state to perform their rituals of divination, healing, and to travel the spiritual world as well as the material world for hunting, and to understand the will of the gods.

Then we discovered a mountainous national preserve and hiked in their beautiful land. Soon we were in Finland and went to Inari where we had learned there might be a woman who could tell us more about the Sámi, the reindeer, and their culture. We found her—a tall, thin, young blonde woman. You, Keith, said, "She looks like a Reindeer Goddess!" Her mother, a traditional Sámi, did believe a white reindeer was a reincarnation of a human being.

We learned the Sámi honor the animals, rocks, trees, plants and other beings of Nature and venerate the dead. The tree of life which unites the underworld, the human Earth, and the heavenly realm, and which reaches up to the North Star, is central to their belief. *Biejjenniejte*, the Sun Goddess, is their mother and she comes to earth to teach the Sámi people if they have forgotten to care for the reindeer and other creatures of the earth. The Sun is a divine force that can heat the land, which becomes freezing during winter, and it can keep humans and other earthly beings warm.

Finally we started back to Helsinki. On the way we took a night ferry and stopped to see the home of Sibelius, the composer of "Finlandia," the music we had heard on Independence Pass where we were inspired to take our first reindeer trip. After the encounter with Sibelius, we went to Helsinki where a great cathedral carved out of rock provided a sacred space for prayer.

We returned home filled with gratitude and love of the holy Sámi people and their reindeer, the mystical animal spirits that guided this part of the trip.

CHAPTER 20

The Pathfinder

On the way home from our first Arctic trip we stopped in Philadelphia to visit my mother and give her some treasures from the Sámi people. She loved a red Sámi dress since it was her favorite color.

Synchronistically, the Norwegian film, *The Pathfinder*, directed by Nils Gaup, a Sámi himself, was playing at a local art theater. *The Pathfinder* was the first film in its native Sámi language to be made and it was nominated for many awards including the Academy Award for best foreign film in 1988. It is based on a 1,000-year-old legend and depicts the story of a young boy who becomes the Pathfinder for his people.

At the film's start, the viewer sees a mysterious vision that the shaman, Raste, saw only three times in his life—once in his youth, once in mid-life, and just before his death—a vision of the majestic and mystical White Reindeer. Raste knows this vision portends a significant event for his people.

Aigin, a sixteen-year-old boy, is skiing home after a hunting trip. In his absence a band of plundering war mongers, the Tchudes, has found and killed his family.

Aigin stops at the crest of a hill and sees the massacre.

They have killed his sister and her dog, and then his parents, pillaged his home, and put the bloody corpses in a hole in the snow.

Horrified, Aigin wants to warn another nearby group of Sámi, but his ski slips and the Tchudes see him. As Aigin flees, the ominous Tchudes, dressed in black metallic armor, chase him, want to kill him, and wound his arm with a crossbow.

Badly hurt, Aigin reaches the other Sámi, but collapses unconscious at the edge of their settlement. Upon awaking, he warns the group to fight the Tchudes, but the peace loving Sámi would rather flee to safety.

While most of the Sámi leave, Aigin rests in a tent. The shaman, Raste, stays with him along with a young girl, Salve, who tends to his wounds, but then must flee with the others.

Aigin tells Raste of his despair and hopelessness.

Raste knows words will not help, but asks Aigin what he sees. In despair, the boy says, "Nothing." Suddenly Raste grabs him from behind and puts his hand over his mouth so he can't breathe.

Then Raste releases him and tells Aigin that the common air they breathe unites all people. The Sámi understand this, know they are all related, and live in peace and harmony. But the warlike Tchudes have lost this unity. They have cut themselves off from humanity and from one another. Raste predicts that this will be their downfall.

Understanding the truth of Raste's story, Aigin recommits to life again. He has also felt the love of Salve who tended to him.

Raste shares his vision of the white reindeer with Aigin, who now experiences the beginning of his journey to be a shaman, a vocation that Raste already has seen for the boy.

Raste gives Aigin his shamanic drum and tells him to keep it hidden until he reaches the next Sámi community. Then he must give the drum to the wise eldest woman.

Just then the Tchudes invade the camp and take Raste and Aigin hostage.

To save Raste's life, Aigin tells the Tchudes that he will take them to the Sámi group. But the Tchudes kill Raste anyway—a fate that the shaman has foreseen.

Aigin tells the Tchudes he will take them the shortest way, knowing that it requires crossing a treacherous route known only to the Sámi; it is their way over the Holy Mountain, Passevari.

Aigin tells the Tchudes that they must tie themselves together with ropes if they want to cross over the mountain. Now they are dependent on Aigin.

As they descend into the abyss below, Aigin suddenly jumps over the edge and holds onto a boulder while the Tchudes try to go down. Aigin takes a knife he has hidden and cuts the rope. The Tchudes cut themselves off from the saving rope, and from one another in their fear, thus destroying their unity as Raste had predicted. An avalanche kills them all and now Aigin makes his own path. As he looks up at the peak of the Holy Mountain he has a vision. A great white reindeer appears and looks powerfully in the eyes of Aigin, then disappears back in the clouds. Although Aigin is not yet aware of his destiny, the vision shows he is a shaman.

Aigin reaches the Sámi camp and tells them they are now safe. Then he hands the drum to the wise elder woman.

She knows he will be the new shaman and hands the drum back to Aigin proclaiming him their Pathfinder.

Keith, this story led us to a deep understanding of the round smiling faces of the peaceful Sámi, who wear soft reindeer fur-lined parkas and who value spontaneity and play, in contrast with the black-metallic mean look of the Tchudes, who want control and power. And from my seeing a scene in the sauna in which the Sámi women gather without clothes and smile and laugh with each other, it showed me that gentleness and vulnerability is a strength that unites them with each other and with Nature. And so, Keith, you and I learned and were united by these Sámi values. And we were even given a gift of *The Pathfinder* film to help hold our memories for us.

CHAPTER 21

Caribou Running, Their Antlers a Sea of Beauty

In 1991 Keith was offered a job to work with the Yupik People of the Yukon Delta in Alaska. The Elders were concerned about the high numbers of deaths from addiction and suicides among their youths. They felt that their spiritual values were on the decline.

Keith's work was to help the Elders in their search to teach the young their values and to help the youths understand how important their spiritual life was to their existence. They couldn't have found a better doctor for this task since Keith and I had been practicing shamanic rituals by building sweat lodges with a Lakota medicine woman. Keith understood how important spiritual practice was to freedom from addiction and suicide. As a very masculine man, he could relate to the young men, and as a deeply spiritual man, he could relate to the Elders. Every day he boarded a small bush plane which took him to the various locations of the Yupik people. Of all his many assignments this was his greatest.

After Keith's job was over I met him in Alaska. We had seen a film, *Never Cry Wolf*, directed by Carrol Ballard. In it were spectacular scenes of caribou running, their antlers a sea of beauty. With this image in mind we wanted to fly over the running caribou to absorb their grandeur.

Caribou are the American cousins of the reindeer. They live in the Arctic, they go on a journey to give birth, and the females have antlers. They are bigger than reindeer.

We flew to Kotzebue, an Inuit town above the Arctic Circle and from there we hired a bush pilot to fly over the Brooks range where forest rangers had spotted a moving herd a day earlier. But we found no caribou that day. We were on a "Fool's Journey" again.

We flew to the Seward Peninsula where we were told we might see both caribou and reindeer. In earlier times reindeer had traveled from Europe to America. But after we arrived in Nome, we learned that the reindeer antlers had been severed. Greedy people knew that when the antlers were covered in velvet they could be sold for huge profit in Asia because they were aphrodisiacs.

We decided to seek solace in Nature. A man whom we met at the airport took us hiking. He was a university professor and a kind and generous man. While hiking we spotted a lone reindeer swimming across a river. Keith also spotted a rack of antlers that lay hidden in a rocky crevice. We treasured this "gift" from our totemic animal to encourage us on our journey. These antlers grace my stove today.

Unlike the reindeer in Europe, the caribou are not followed by their people. Instead, each stage of the caribou's journey is marked on the calendar by the tribal groups that honor them. Each month is marked by the location of the caribou and their link with the moon cycles. For example, there is the "Moon of the Old Bucks," the "Moon of the Cold Udders," the "Full Udder Moon," the "Moon of the Calves," the "Moon of the Waters," the "Moon of the Fall Leaves," and so on. Knowing the caribou location by the Time of the Moon allows tribe members to track and hunt them.

The lives of the caribou and their people are threatened by huge companies who want to drill for oil with no regard for the caribou migration path. This is a sort of "ethnic cleansing," an indigenous woman told us. "If the caribou die when their migration routes are bought and destroyed for greedy oil companies, our population will die, too."

We left Alaska with great admiration for the caribou, their followers, and the majesty of their land. But also we shed tears for the threat to their existence.

CHAPTER 22

Creation's Heartbeat

Linda: Keith, I found my favorite creation story of the world and its sacred reindeer. Right here, in my notes! It describes the beautiful Sun Goddess, *Biejjenniejte*, who comes to us sometimes in the form of a reindeer to teach us how to be better loving humans. We need only listen to the reindeer's heart that beats at the earth's center… Oh, here, let's read it!

***

Once while walking in solitude by the eternal waters, the creator, Jubmel, found the peace disturbed by evil spirits. Mocking cries, shrieks of hatred, and evil chants invaded the calm of the eternal void. Disturbed, Jubmel decided to create a new world, a universe so peaceful and harmonious that love and compassion would reign and the evil spirits would flee. He wanted the beautiful body of his favorite creature, a gentle reindeer doe, to be the matter from which the new world would be shaped and he wanted her loving heart to inform the new creation.

So he called to the lovely vaja, the reindeer doe, from Passevari, the holy mountain where she grazed. As the radiant doe came running, her golden hooves sparkled lightning shafts of sunlight, delighting the creator's heart.

Turning to the gentle vaja, and looking into her tender eyes, Jubmel said "You, my little vaja, have infinite sadness in your eyes and from your body I will shape the world to set the home of holiness apart from the nether regions."

So the creator took a tiny bone from the body of the reindeer doe and built a bridge that spanned the abyss between his light world and the nether regions.

The innermost structure of the new earth was fashioned from the vaja's bones and became the rocks and boulders and the peaks and mountain ridges. Her flesh became the fertile soil, and her blood and veins the flowing rivers. From her hair the mysterious forests were created. Her skull became the sky which shields the earth from the blazing brightness of the holy heavens. And there the deer's deep, sad eyes became the morning and evening stars to guide the song makers, the dreamers, and the parted lovers and to give them hope.

Finally, Jubmel hid the vaja's still beating heart in the center-most depths of the earth to remind the lost wanderer, the lonely mountaineer, and all those in sorrow, that help would always be there. The vaja's heart would be the heartbeat for the earth, so that when peace and love reigned the reindeer doe's heart would beat with joy. But if hatred and greed disrupted the earth's harmony, her heart would convulse in pain and tremors would shake the earth from top to bottom.

The beauty of the new earth was abundant. Sweet milk—the holy milk of the vaja—flowed forth from the rivers. The tree trunks were filled with marrow, and cheese fruit and meat fruit hung from the branches of the birch and the firs.

Jubmel asked the Sun to shine upon this wondrous creation, and the splendid world created from the body of the gentle doe was so warm and loving that the evil spirits could not approach it.

Delighted with the new world, Jubmel wanted to share his joy, so he created new beings to rejoice on the earth. Jubmel shaped mankind to care for the earth and its gifts. The only commandment Jubmel gave was not to hate.

He created a man and woman to give birth to a race of happy people—the Sámi.

But eventually greed and jealousy consumed one of the new beings who took the good things from the earth and forgot to thank the new creation.

The wickedness of the greedy caused the vaja's heart to beat with pain and terror until the earth quaked and people fell into the earth's chasms!

Jubmel decided to hide all the treasures of the earth near the heart of the vaja. If the vaja's heart beat with joy, then Jubmel would know all was good. But if the reindeer doe's heart beat with sorrow and terror, he would know evil spirits prevailed.

Jubmel brought forth the Sun Goddess, *Biejjenniejte*—born from a beautiful smile and a tear of joy—to shine upon the earth and to dwell there to teach the people how to care for the reindeer and the other blessings of the earth. Sometimes she came in the form of the reindeer to teach the ways of goodness and humility, and she taught songs of the shaman who then could remind the people and guide them with their magic drums to listen to the holy vaja's heartbeats. For near the doe's loving heart the treasures of the earth were saved. And so the gentle reindeer doe became Creation's Heartbeat.

***

Keith: A lovely story with much wonder.

CHAPTER 23

Siberia, Synchronicity, and Reindeer

Now it was time for our third journey to reindeer land. I read that tribes in Siberia honored the reindeer and believed they were on earth to care for them. The adventurer and writer, Farley Mowat, travelled to Siberia to be with them. So I decided to arrange a trip for Keith and myself to visit our totem animals in distant Siberia.

Following an Impossible Dream

I was told that such a trip was impossible. Finally I contacted a Russian travel agency, but they also said it was impossible. Still I knew Farley Mowat had been there. I wouldn't give up so easily.

During a meal with my good friend and colleague, Betty Meador, I mentioned my wish to go to Siberia. She told me that a Siberian woman was visiting her brother-in-law; perhaps I could talk to her. What luck! When I called her, she said that her husband, a scientist in Novosibirsk, had arranged a trip for therapists the previous year. I contacted him and he said he could arrange a Siberian trip. It would take sending him a lot of money in cash and getting the required visas. He hadn't heard of Reindeer people, but he would research where they might be.

How to find the Reindeer people would be a challenge!

About this time I went to Pacifica graduate school to lecture on my addiction and creativity book. I mentioned my desire to go to Siberia to the chairman, Jonathon, who told me he had gone from Alaska to a part of Siberia along the coast. As we were talking, a young woman came to his office. She told him she was studying shamanism and had heard there was a conference on shamanism in Siberia perhaps near Lake Baikal. I could hardly believe this good news. Now I had a lead for the Siberian scientist to follow.

Synchronicities have always been part of my life—those meaningful events in which a happening in the external world corresponds to an internal quest, but are not causally related. Fate was on my side. Finding the Reindeer people now seemed possible, and a call meant to come true.

Immediately I contacted the scientist from Novosibirsk. With this information, he thought he could track down where the conference was held and even locate the tribe. He learned that the conference would be in Yakutsk in August and that a scholar related to the Even tribe would be attending it. The Evens were one of several groups devoted to caring for the reindeer.

Faith was required to make this journey. Sending a large amount of cash to someone we didn't know was not easy for us. I had quit my major source of income from seeing clients because I wanted to devote my time to writing. I was making ends meet from limited royalties. Keith had quit his steady job at Napa; he was sixty-eight and now had income from temporary jobs as a psychiatrist through *locum tenens* assignments. Neither of us came from wealthy families; my family was poor and Keith's sister had inherited his parent's funds. Knowing we might lose all our money was a risk we had to make if we wanted to take this trip. Would this be another "Fool's Journey?" Or would it be the adventure of a lifetime?

We decided to take the chance. This opportunity had come, after all, from an acquaintance of my friend, Betty Meador, a wonderful woman.

How we might actually travel in Siberia was a question we had not considered. Later, when faced with this reality, we were amazed at our naivety. But we were both adventurers who enjoyed meeting the unknown.

Sharing a Dream of Freedom

Before going to Russia, I was invited to lecture at a Transpersonal Psychology conference in Prague. I gave a lecture that featured a dream about a Reindeer Goddess that Keith had, titled "The Reindeer Woman in the World's Dark Night."

After my talk, a young Czechoslovakian woman came up to me in tears. Stifled by the oppressive regime in her communist country, she had dreams and images of herself riding a reindeer to freedom. Keith's dream was a living example that her own image was not confined to herself alone. Her mother had read her the fairy tale of the Snow Queen, in which a young girl rides a reindeer to free a boy from imprisonment by the Ice Queen, just as she felt hostage to the Soviet system in her native country. She had used this image to gain inner freedom for her life. With Keith's dream she had confirmation that she was not alone. The fact that female reindeer have antlers to protect themselves on their journey to give birth gave her additional support to protect her soul's integrity in the face of living in a freezing totalitarian state.

First Steps Toward Russia

Afterward Keith and I spent a few days in Budapest and then in Vienna. We travelled to important sites in Poland, including to Krakow and Auschwitz to witness what was left of the Holocaust extermination camp. We felt a moral imperative to witness the horror of the camp.

Finally we boarded a train to Kiev in Ukraine where we were to meet our Russian guides. While boarding the train, Keith was robbed by pickpockets, but they did not get all of his money. We were in a sleeper compartment in which two huge men also had bunks. We looked at each other wondering if we would be safe from these men, but they smiled and all was well. Finally we arrived at Kiev and met up with our Russian guides. Kiev was very beautiful and had an astounding monastery. We stood in the park that is now decimated from the Russian-Ukrainian war.

In Kiev we were met by our Russian translator, Galina Bukova, and our guide, Ivan. Our first meeting with Yuri Osipov, the scientist who arranged our trip, would be in his home in Novisibirsk, Siberia.

Meeting Russians As They Live

We began to understand why we had to send so much cash before our arrival. Plane fares were different for native Russians than for foreigners, who paid astronomically higher amounts for tickets. Boarding a plane was also unlike anything we had previously encountered. When the plane doors opened crowds of Russians rushed in crushing those around them. Our guides paid for our rides in cash and managed to get us seats. With luck the plane would have enough fuel to fly. But, if there was no fuel, the passengers had to wait. Many times we had to fly back to Moscow, wait in the airport sometimes for days, then finally fly to a Siberian destination.

The period in Russia was 1992; a transition time from Soviet rule to a more open jurisdiction. In 1991 Gorbachev had instituted changes that allowed more freedom. Initially he adhered to Marxism-Leninism but moved to social democracy. His policy of *glasnost* (*openness*) enabled freedom of speech and press; his policy of *perestroika* (*restructuring*) attempted to decentralize economic decision-making for efficiency.

Since Russia had become more open, it enabled Keith and I to travel, though we had to have visas for various provinces with clearly demarcated dates. We accepted confusing ways of traveling as part of our trip to the reindeer land.

We met up with our cordial trip planner, Yuri Osipov, who was warm and welcoming. He arranged dinners in homes with intellectuals and some wonderful surprises for our journey. We loved being with him. We also loved our translator, Galina, and admired our guides, Ivan and Illusha. How lucky we were to be shown high points of Siberia personally and with so much care. Yuri had arranged for us to go to Ulan-Use, a city near Mongolia, to visit a Tibetan temple that had shamanic influences. I remember seeing a sacred tree with white prayer cloths on its branches. We sat gratefully in the temple with the monks.

Most striking was our visit to Lake Baikal, an ancient lake considered to be one of the deepest and most clearest lakes in the world. Our guides took us to an area many miles away from the entrance to the lake. They initiated us with a sauna in which, at the end of the heating process, they "beat" us with branches from a birch tree. Then that evening we were taken to a special boat in which we could make love as it floated gently back to the entrance shore. This was a "night sea journey" never to be forgotten. Natives believe there is an "invisible city" at the bottom of the lake. We had seen a film by Werner Herzog about this invisible city—a mystical home for believers like ourselves.

By now we knew how desperate the Russian people were. We experienced their despair, the unpredictability of their lives, the pollution of their land, and the shrinking of their rubles. We had to travel from Ulan-Ude all the way back to Moscow. There we waited several days in the airport to catch a plane to Yakutsk, where another plane was supposed to take us to the Even tribe who rode the reindeer. Keith joked in a whisper that with conditions in Russia so dire, we had at least saved money for a hotel as we lay waiting on the airport floor. We were already a day late and feared the plane in Yakutsk had left. We had to give up all our Western notions about control.

Taking a Russian Helicopter to Reindeer Country

Finally we did get to Yakutsk where the drinking water was so green and polluted that even boiling it didn't seem safe. But, miraculously the plane to reindeer country was there. We boarded a former Soviet military helicopter to find only sacks of potatoes on which to sit. Two local women were on the helicopter along with a suspicious looking local man. We were happy to have the potato seats. Our translator and guide were with us, too.

After about two-and-a-half hours flying, the helicopter swooped down, landing in a dry river bed. Our guides got out and motioned to us to get out, too. The local man also got out and some men came running to the plane to give the pilot slabs of meat. Then the helicopter took off leaving us in an eerie Arctic wild land. We looked at the helicopter flying away and wondered if it would return for us. We were in the remote mountainous land by the Lena River and the Arctic Circle. We wondered if it was safe to be near this local man, but he motioned to us to climb up a hill where we were greeted by an Elder tribesman.

Greeted by the Elder and Running Reindeer

The Elder grinned and pointed in the distance. There hundreds of reindeer were running toward us with a sea of antlers which looked like birch branches waving in the wind. Their hooves thundered on the turf and we heard their grunts to each other. Yes, we had arrived at the temporary camping place for Even people riding with their reindeer.

But who was this strange local man and why was he with us on the helicopter? Our translator, Galina, explained that he was a member of the Even tribe, but also a professor in Yakutsk where the Shaman conference was to be held. It was he who had found a way to bring us to the Even people. He would translate the elder's language into Russian; then Galina would translate what he said into English.

The Even are one of the most ancient tribes who revere the reindeer. Now they have become one of the smallest groups of reindeer people. They are hunters and fishers as well as nomadic reindeer herders. The Elder, a short round man of seventy, emanated a serenity that reminded us of the Buddha. He explained that the souls of the people and the reindeer are inter-related and interdependent. They need each other. Each Even person has a particular reindeer to which they are related. When an Even person dies his body is placed high in tree branches along with the antlers of his special reindeer. Then the reindeer flies to the Spirit World taking the Even person with it. The Elder pointed to a tree saying it was the embodiment of the World Tree or Tree of Life and that the reindeer antlers comprised its branches. From the leafy sacred cradle of the World Tree the souls of the Even and the reindeer ride together in the Spirit World.

The Even People Are Reindeer

Without a personal reindeer, an Even person is not a human being, since the Even is half-human and half-reindeer. The Even believe they are reindeer, which allows the reindeer to show them the best pastures and whether they are allowed to hunt. Reindeer communicate with divine forces—with the mountains, rivers, and the winds—so they know where the animals are. The Even believe the reindeer will carry them into the future; thus they are worried about the reindeer's fate since their existence and their habitat are threatened by pollution.

When the Soviets were in power, they forced the children to leave their beautiful wild home and to go away to school to learn the Russian language and Soviet ways. Many of these Even stayed in cities and forgot about the reindeer and how to care for them. The Even were also confined to certain districts and not allowed to travel, thus frustrating their nomadic life which is to roam with the reindeer.

Earlier, shamans communicated between the reindeer and the people. But after the 1917 revolution, many shamans were killed, and if they escaped, they had to hide their visions and rituals, therefore depriving them and the people of their healing and wisdom. Sadly the Elder confided that he did not know as much about caring for the reindeer as his father, and that he feared that his children would not know the reindeer ways as well as himself.

We learned these truths as we sat around the campfire with the Elder speaking to us.

Meeting the Even

The Even believe they were created to ride the reindeer. They do so with the help of a long pole which they use to guide their mounts and for balance atop their animal's uneven gait. The pole is a manifestation of the world tree that unites the three places of reality—the upper world of spirit, the mid-world of earth, and the underworld. The pole gives them a supernatural center of balance through which they experience an ecstatic state of serenity; thus riding the reindeer is a spiritual force.

Our Elder said, "The reindeer is a child of the sun and turns into a great swan as it flies to the sun, which is its home. A golden reindeer pulls the sun across the sky. When we ride the reindeer, we fly like birds. To us the reindeer is like a great spaceship, a bird that is always in the air."

As we lived with the Even people, listened to their mystical wisdom, drank the holy milk of the reindeer doe, ate its meat, and even tasted its warm blood, we drifted into another sense of time and space. We climbed the mountains of the valley, walked along high ridges, and felt the warm touch of the sun, their mother, on our skin. And our hearts were caressed by these soulful people, by the reindeer, and by Nature's generosity. We saw the vibrant colors of the late summer tundra—the muted green and golden moss, the red and golden bushes, and the lavender lichen-covered grey rocks—intermingled with the ever-swaying antlers of the holy deer.

Keith Sees the Reindeer Goddess

On the afternoon of our arrival, Keith went hiking along the ridge of the Even camp, and he had a vision of the same Reindeer Woman he had once seen in his dream before this trip. He knelt down and bowed to honor Her. The next day he told the Even Elder of his vision. We had already told him of Keith's earlier dream that launched our trip when the Elder asked why we had come to visit. Thus far they had only ever experienced two other visitors—two hunters and a BBC team to film them.

Keith's recent dream vision was taken as one of their own, since they worshipped a Reindeer Goddess whose name "Khinken" meant "without stress," and who protected all living beings. When she appears in an Even's dreams, it is a sign that she has granted them permission to hunt. Although the Even did not tell us, they knew that they would be successful in their hunt that night.

It was so cold that night that I arose early to warm myself by the campfire. Three severed, bloody heads of Bighorn sheep lay before the fire and I stepped back alarmed by the sight. But then I saw the Elder smiling to tell me that this was good. I understood that this was part of an organic whole. The chief hunter said that Keith's dream and vision of the Reindeer Goddess had given them permission to hunt that night. The reindeer took them to the place where the bighorn sheep were grazing and offered themselves up to be taken.

Our time around the campfire listening to the Elder was when we also ate. A stick with cooked meat on it would be passed around the fire. Each person took only the meat he would eat and then passed it on to the next one. When everyone had been served, a new stick with meat was passed around. In this way no more food was taken than what was needed.

The value of conservation for the survival of everyone was upheld in this way.

Riding the Reindeer—Well Almost

The Even people were playful. They asked Keith and myself if we would like to ride the reindeer. Never to turn down an opportunity to learn, we both said yes. Once astride a reindeer with a sort of rope bridle, we were given the pole by which to balance. The reindeer started off with their unusual, uneven gait. I lasted only a few steps before being thrown off and onto the ground. The Evens laughed at our unsuccessful attempts. I tried a few times, but each time I fell. Keith, too, had the same experience. Their laughter was like a child's, good-natured and fun. Here again we became the "Fool," and we laughed with them at ourselves.

One day the Elder asked Keith to help him; we had told him Keith was a doctor. The Elder asked Keith to check his heart since it would be a long time until he was able to see a doctor in Yakutsk. Keith nodded and checked the Elder's chest and back carefully, then told him all was good. In thanks the Elder gave Keith a bloody bear paw and a necklace of what seemed to be kidney stones. Keith accepted these gratefully. Later I wondered if the Elder had somehow sensed a heart condition that Keith suffered and had given Keith these precious offerings to help him in times of need.

On the day we left the Even, the Elder told us: "We are glad that Russia and America are now peaceful friends. We managed to survive the Soviet period since we live far away in the wilds.

In our language we do not use the word 'kill' because it means to kill the soul. We believe that all peoples have different ways to find the path to the spirit and that each way, though different, is good, just as the different cells in the body are good."

Living Our Shangri-La Dreams

When preparing for us to leave, I had a secret wish that the helicopter would not come so we could spend more time in this Siberian Shangri-La. I did not want to leave the Elder or the gentle Even people. Most of all I didn't want to leave the reindeer with their beautiful soulful eyes and their antlered crowns raised up to other worlds in the heavenly skies. But I knew that, whether or not I returned, I had their beauty engraved deeply in my heart. I also felt that the reindeer and the people who revere them would be visiting in my dreams. And I hoped to share my experience of these peaceful beings with others, just as stories are passed down through the generations.

Keith: Linda, I realize now, as you retell our story, I had a dream—and it became part of our journey. And the Even people learned of my dream, believed, and it led to a successful hunt. Linda, in this our adventure, my dreams came true!

PART 3

From the Wings of Angels

"I am circling around God,
around the ancient tower
I have been circling for a
Thousand years and I still
don't know if I am a falcon: or
a storm, or a great song"

—Rainer Maria Rilke

Postcard of an angel received by Linda.

CHAPTER 24

Two Birds Flying

Linda: Sweetheart, you told me many times that you always sign your letters to me with the sign for "Two Birds Flying" because it symbolizes two soulmates flying free together in the heavens on a spiritual adventure. You love birds and had a special bird book which you read often. The signs remind me of the emoji with two hearts, one leading the way. Two Birds Flying was your imprint on me, on us, and on our hearts.

When we were in Santa Fe, where I was giving a seminar on my book, *On the Way to the Wedding*, a Sufi woman came up to me and offered me a free massage in thanks for the book. While she was massaging me a most remarkable thing happened. Suddenly a great white Angel Wing like the one Rilke describes in The *Duino Elegies* sprouted right out of my left shoulder blade. I could both see it and sense it coming out of my body, an overwhelming physical experience. Rilke's great poetic cycle deepened our soulmate relationship and the poems called out to the majestic Angel to hear us and protect us in times of despair while we were on our flight to the Divine Wedding.

Later, while giving a lecture at Esalen, I had a massage by a young woman from Hawaii. During this massage I had another Wing come out of my body—this time from the shoulder blade on the right side. This wing was a huge powerful eagle wing; again I could both see it and feel it physically emerge. Since we were on Native American soil, I experienced it as a testament to the sweat lodge rituals we had practiced at the annual shamanic weekends at Winter Park, Colorado guided by our analyst, Don Sandner. He had arranged for Pansy Hawkwing and her son from the Lakota Reservation in the Dakotas to teach us how to gather tree limbs, branches, soil and grass, to build the sweat lodge. Then she taught us how to prepare the burning coals and to stay and pray to the *Great Spirit* during the sweltering heat which enabled the toxins in body and psyche to clear out to leave us pure.

CHAPTER 25

Back to the Sacred Garden

Linda: Sweetheart, I had a dream last night that I feel you sent me from afar and that helps me believe you are in a heavenly home.

In the dream we were staying in a hotel on the corner of a street in an unknown city. We went across the street to a cafe for breakfast and were seated at a table with vividly colored flowers, so many and so tall and lush that they were breathtaking. The flowers were deep purple, rose red, crimson, and royal blue and some were magenta, fuchsia, orange and golden and bright yellow like the sun. The table was like a garden with the flowers, so many and so high, they towered above us. We were in a veritable Garden of Eden, a Paradise in which Adam and Eve dwelled before succumbing to the temptations of the fallen Angel, Lucifer.

When I awoke, I was in awe and felt that you were showing me that you were safe and in grace in a transcendent realm awaiting for me to join you when it was my time to come. Sweetheart, I love you so much.

CHAPTER 26

Charming Keith's Sacred Fool

Jean Le Fou (opening the door): Oh good morning, Linda! So good to see you. Come in, come in. Let me make you a cup of coffee. It's been weeks since I've seen you. Two sugars, as always?

On the phone you mentioned you had a wonderful reveal of an Angel's wing on your shoulder! Few people meet themselves with wings! You'll have to show old Jean Le Fou those wings sometime. I'm glad your wings aren't out right now or you couldn't walk through my door!

And you mentioned a grand and important thing about your charming Keith. You said a successful part of him was being a happy Fool. I know the Fool, it is my favorite tarot card.

Here is your coffee, two sugars. Milk?

Now tell me how Keith, your love, was among so many things, a laughing and open Fool! Tell me of Keith's journeys as a happy wonderer, a Fool—open, laughing, fallen, but always rising with a laugh. He was so caring. Your Jean here needs to hear more.

Linda: Nice to see you again. Jean, I'm just back from the concert by Gil Shaham, the violinist who I told you came over to talk to Keith at the rich folks house in Aspen; he played Brahm's Violin concerto—my favorite violin concerto of all. He was just as good and personable as when he was younger some thirty years ago! Then the orchestra played *Shostakovich* —a stirring Russian symphony. My friend got tickets not knowing how much personal connection I had to those musical pieces. So Keith was at this concert with me! It felt so wonderful. My friend loved the concert, too.

Jean: So the music brought him there with you again.

Linda: So much so, I had a dream of him last night. May I tell you?

Up in the sky is a beautiful cloud. I look and see Keith's face, large and smiling at me. Then slowly the cloud begins to disappear and Keith's face fades with the cloud. It reminds me of a fan painted by Oscar Kokoschka, a depiction of his torrid love affair for Alma Mahler. He painted seven fans for her as "love letters in pictorial form," painted on the occasion of Alma's birthday. Each fan depicted their secret love affair, one with the lovers seeking shelter in a boat, in the background is Vesuvius erupting. A fan as a love letter to Alma Mahler, a muse Keith and I admired. And in my dream, the fan slowly closes in the sky… Until Keith's face is no longer there. It is an image of my longing for him, that I still carry like a imaginary fan to this day.

Jean: How beautiful, poetic, that dream; his face as a love letter in the sky.

Linda: Yes, Keith, he did love poetry, especially Rilke's *Duino Elegies*—which he felt was the greatest poetic cycle ever written. Keith and I spent a lot of time reading Rilke.

Keith went with me to Robert Bly's conference on the "Wild Man" in the woods and Keith was the only real wild man there. A woman got sick there from drinking too much and Keith took care of her and arranged to get her to a hospital. So Bly saw Keith as healer and also as Wild Man and was drawn to him as many creative people were. Bly befriended Keith—and even stroked Keith's cheek and beard fondly whenever they met. I also think that Bly's affection towards Keith was a sign to me that Bly thought I had found a good partner.

Jean: Chance friendships like that are the gift to the open-hearted Fool.

Linda: Oh, but he wasn't always mild-mannered. If need be, he could be ferocious, protecting patients and others from harm. But the Fool part of him was tender-hearted, and his patients felt his care and love. The Fool was a strong figure in Keith's work with psychotics. It enabled him to go deep in the abyss of the psyche so that the patients weren't threatened, because they could feel he understood them and their crazy behaviors. Keith wasn't afraid; he'd been there too.

Jean: Linda, the Fool walks enthusiastic, delighted to find the new, but in their enjoyment, it can possess them, cause them to make mistakes. They may start a journey with a fall. Did you see that in Keith, falls that must be recovered from?

Linda (laughing): Oh yes. Once I remember we were on a boat in the Amazon, Brazil, and it was time to go ashore at Macau. Keith was ebullient, in a hurry to be first to go down the gangplank to see the unique Opera House. Laughing, he strode out with a grandiose gesture and wave to all, and stepped off the gangplank and landed on his face in the water. All the waiting passengers saw his fall. He was able to laugh at himself as he picked himself up. Luckily he wasn't hurt.

And Jean, I remember another fall of Keith's. A bit more serious. One that involved a naïveté at a workshop I was giving on addiction at the Omega Institute. Keith shared that he had a drinking problem and the participants, who were mostly children of alcoholics, became enraged. But a man sitting next to us stood up and gave Keith a hug; he was an alcoholic who was actually in charge of the Bill W. House. Alcoholics learn to laugh at themselves for the foolish things they do when drunk. So this turned out well for Keith. His faux pas passed. But Omega administers told me they would not invite me to lecture there again. I wasn't angry at Keith, because I knew he admitted his drinking with a good heart and did not know how injured and resentful the workshop people were. I was grateful for the man who gave Keith an AA hug.

I can say the Fool is usually present at AA meetings where there is a lot of laughter—because it is very healing to be able to admit to mistakes and laugh at oneself—a Fool among many others.

Jean: Two fools meet and there is forgiveness. Fools often are resilient, and after their fall, they begin a new journey. To find themselves in a new place.

Linda: Yes, I've seen that in Keith, in another incident of outlandish Fool behavior. As a couple, two adventurers he and I, we went to climb Kilimanjaro. Keith was very excited by the climb. So excited that he left our climbing group to climb on his own, alone, like the famous African explorer, Livingston, climbing through the jungle alone. He was so proud to be climbing Kilimanjaro, he was acting the complete Fool.

Jean: Did he later experience the Fool's fall?

Linda: Yes. I was angry with him. As we ascended near the top, at high elevation, Keith suddenly was stumbling, with altitude sickness. The leader ordered him down the mountain. And I wondered how Keith would take finding he could not finish the climb.

But something miraculous happened: Keith remembered a dream about going around the mountain on circular stones. The stones had symbols that Keith was to understand. And using them, he rose above his anger, saw himself there on mountain, and was happy to master himself. He was not angry. And I truly loved him for that!

Jean: That is the Fool, fall, rise again, resilient, and begin a new journey to find yourself. And this, he did. *Formidable! Voila, Le Fou!*

Now, Linda, my friend with wings. Let me draw a card for you. We always have fun talking the cards. Come on! Be Linda, Keith's Angel with wings! Here, I draw this card for you:

The Magus!

Wonderful, Linda, this is really you. The Magus, or Magician, represents your talents, your capabilities for success. We start as a Fool, and learn, become ourselves, and then… We master our being. The Magus represents your capabilities to do, to travel, to know as master of your world. So Linda, feel this truth about you. You climbed Kilimanjaro, you learn philosophy and psychoanalysis as if they are simple water you drink. You love a magnificent Fool. Now honor this Magus in you, your legacy.

To you, Linda, I say, "*Bien Fait!*"

Linda: Well, thank you, Jean. Fun to see you as always.

CHAPTER 27

Ayn Rand-Freed by an Author

Keith: Linda, you told me how hard it was to leave your mother in order to be free to live your own life. Did anyone help you?

Linda: My mother wanted me to stay in Philadelphia to help her with my father. But I was feeling stifled like I was in a prison cell. If I did leave though, I would feel guilty. A friend suggested I read *The Fountainhead* by Ayn Rand, who was a popular author for my generation in the 1950s. I also read her next novel, *Atlas Shrugged.*

I was liberated by Rand's central idea—to live by following one's own creative call. Rand had grown up in Soviet Russia where she could not be free. Her father's store had been confiscated. She knew she had to leave Russia to be free. She saw the Soviet regime as parasitic. She left, immigrated to the United States, and built a new life for herself.

I realized that my mother's claim on my life was parasitic.

Rand's insistence that the meaning of being human was to create, and not to follow, gave me permission to discover myself. While I later disagreed with her political and economic views, her early influence gave me a way to start on my own path.

CHAPTER 28

My Professional Path

Keith: Dear Heart. Tell me again how you designed your three different jobs. Did it take lots of planning?

Linda: Really I did not plan them. They just sprouted up and one led to another. I'll tell you again as much as I know for it amazes me, too.

As you know I grew up in a poor alcoholic home. My only plan was that I would get out, so I could be myself, whoever that was. My grandmother taught and encouraged me to read. And actually my father encouraged me, too. My mother did not but she taught me how to work hard.

Luckily, I was bright. And I loved to learn. I was skipped a year in elementary school. In high school I was especially good in mathematics and physics, and I loved my math teacher, Mr. Cohen, so I majored in math in college. I won several scholarships and those, combined with a number of jobs, enabled me to go to Temple University, the city college for poor people. By junior year, I was bored with math and I wasn't good at making three-dimensional charts. A friend, who majored in journalism, suggested I switch my major to the same, and I did. Thank God for that.

At the start I thought I would like to write features on different cultures for magazines. The department chairman, Mr. Perry, suggested starting out as a reporter on a newspaper. I really liked this idea and saw in it a way to get away from home. So I wrote a hundred applications to newspapers in the mountain states, and also to Hawaii and Alaska. A paper in Ketchikan, Alaska offered me a job, but I couldn't get there fast enough, so I lost that job to another. Mr. Perry suggested I write again, but include my picture. I did this and received six offers and I chose the job in Cañon City, Colorado. I had always wanted to live in the Rocky Mountains, because my grandmother's dream was to see those majestic peaks lifting to the sky.

My mother didn't want me to go, but she agreed to help me drive there. On the way she accidentally drove the car off the road due to construction work. So we both ended up in the hospital; fortunately we were not hurt too badly. But I had one huge black eye and had to call the newspaper to say I would be late. The black eye turned out to be an advantage; it broke the ice. The editor had no idea what I was like and wondered what a big city girl from the east would be like. But when I arrived, we all had a big laugh. The black eye also helped with my interviews for my work as a reporter on a small daily. The firemen especially teased me a lot; I loved to visit them on my daily rounds.

Cañon City lies on the Arkansas River and is at the foot of the mountains. It housed the state prison where many people worked, and was home to the great Royal Gorge which was spanned by a high rickety bridge that few dared to cross over. Cañon City had a "main drag" which was a street of several blocks that cut through the town. People there were simple, and many were ranchers and workmen.

The newspaper office housed the owner and publisher, Don Hardy, known all over the state for his good will. The city editor, Willes, was like the ones you read about—gruff on the outside while inside was a tender heart. He liked to give me a hard time, but I knew he liked me. The office was rounded out by two advertising men and a secretary, Alice, who became my best friend, and in the back were the printers who ran the press. The paper came out every day and the presses would roll exactly by three p.m. Then we would all go to the five-and-dime for chocolate sundaes and might have coffee. Back again we would finish the day unless there was something special happening. More often than not, I would come back at night to work with the editor and get a head start for the next day.

My "beat" started early. I made daily rounds to the police, the firemen, the sheriff, the county clerk, the head of education, and even the librarian. I walked to all these places and loved my job. If someone special was coming to town, I was sent to interview them. I was not allowed to go to the worst parts of the prison; Willes wanted to protect me, although I, myself, wanted to see what went on in this forbidden area.

Linda's Mother: Oh Linda, my Linda, can you hear me? I'm calling now, from your past. I have something to say to you, from so long ago. I did not want you to go to your new job, but it was important to you that you survive and carry on for yourself. There were so many things I couldn't give. Security, a calm home, a life without fear of your father's drinking. I was afraid. I had to protect you, make you strong. But I was alone. I wanted you with me. You were a beautiful daughter, your tried so hard. And when you went to this job, I had two very hard things to do: I had to help you get to this job. And I had to let you go. Let you leave me for more, for a better world, for a better Self. I'm so so sorry for that accident. It wounded you, and harmed your chances. Linda, I cried. Cried for what I did. Can you forgive me? You do know… I loved you.

Young Linda in 1972.

CHAPTER 29

The Lovers Reversed

Jean: Linda! So glad you came. I've been looking forward to our talks. Always astounding.

Before you came, I drew a card for you. You know me, I can't resist.

The Lovers

Which normally is a wonderful card, about the two sides of our inner world and love intertwining, becoming strong, and then offering love to those around.

But today, The Lovers is reversed. I caught my breath a little. It means trouble in the love department.

Linda, Dear Angel with Wings, have you experienced unrequited loved? Do you want to talk about it?

Linda: Ah yes, it happened in Cañon City, where I was working as a news reporter. Oh I enjoyed that job, and the people I met and interviewed. And one was a man I'll call Mr. X.

Writing the special event stories was my favorite task. I did a feature on a glass blower artist who was in town for a few days. When the prison created a retreat center for convicts about to be released, so they could transition to the outside world safely, I was assigned to interview these men. Perhaps my favorite feature was about a cattle drive on which the ranchers invited me to accompany them. I rode over the hills with them on my horse Snooks. The ranchers also invited me to write about the branding process, in which young calves underwent the steaming hot iron on their flesh, so that each rancher could identify the calves that belonged to them.

But a life changing interview with the architect who designed the controversial new courthouse for Cañon City changed my life forever. And it demarcated the start of a new career. The architect, Mr. X, was influenced by Frank Lloyd Wright. X's designs wedded the buildings to the Nature which surrounded them. His works were truly works of art. My first interview with this creative artist occurred over coffee in a cafe. As I took notes for the article, suddenly I felt a hand upon my knee. It was as though a lightning bolt from Heaven infused my body; it was my first erotic experience. At the time I was young for my age and had not really dated during adolescence. I fell head over heels in love with this creative genius.

Mr. X came to town every few weeks to follow the building of the courthouse. We dated several times. The staff at the newspaper knew how much in love I was with him. One day the ad men took me aside. They had learned that Mr. X was married and told me so in their hopes to protect me. I fell into a great despair. When next I saw Mr. X, I asked him if he was married. Reluctantly he answered, "Yes." I told him I couldn't continue the relationship. He understood and wrote me a soulful letter of apology—a letter I keep by my side after all these years.

Now in despair, I turned to books that might help me deal with all the pain. Someone suggested reading Kierkegaard since he wrote about despair in his treatise *Sickness Unto Death.* As I read the Danish philosopher's words I realized I needed further training to find the layers of meaning embedded in his analysis of despair. And thus was began my second career in philosophy; I enrolled at the University of Colorado in their master's program in philosophy.

I moved to Boulder for this program. I also arranged to get a job as secretary at X's firm! I thought that seeing him in this light, by working for him, I could see his bad points and in this way my overwhelming attraction to him might disappear. The architecture firm had four architects: X, Linden, Nick, and Mack. I went out for coffee with them. And I did discover Mr. X had other women in his life in addition to his wife. I was still in love with him, but managed to alleviate it while working for him. I also delved more deeply into Kierkegaard's analysis of despair.

Jean: Oh, Linda, that is the very meaning of unrequited love. It brought you a new future, philosophy, but with a dear cost.

Linda with her beloved horse Snooks.

CHAPTER 30

Cañon City Rodeo Queen-Almost!

Linda: Soon after arriving in Cañon City I bought two treasured belongings with my first paychecks. One was a horse and the other was a pair of skis.

A cowboy I met offered to purchase a horse for me from North Dakota on one of his trips to buy and sell horses. Snooks, the name I chose for him, was a black older gelding of mixed quarter horse stock, a sturdy steed with a mind of his own, more often than not trying to take the reins away from me.

Sometimes I rode him into town to show the firemen. When they saw Snooks they laughed and said, "That animal is so old his lips touch the ground." The firemen never ceased to tease me.

I boarded Snooks at the Benedictine Abbey just east of town, a large area where I could ride and where monks took care of the horses. On days I didn't work, I rode Snooks up the rugged dirt road to Phantom Canyon, where I would stop for lunch, let Snooks graze, and read Thoreau's *Walden*, an inspiring book of insight about living and walking in Nature. My grandmother, who had always talked about wanting to see the Rocky Mountains, had read this book to me when I was a child. So Snooks, my grandmother and her dream of the mountains, and the words of wisdom from *Walden* fit perfectly together in Phantom Canyon, where spirits were said to haunt the place.

Father Leonard Schwinn was the abbot of the monastery. He influenced my life deeply. And he taught extension courses on philosophy for the University of Colorado. He was a tall, handsome, white-haired man most probably in his seventies, a sage and contemplative thinker. Father Schwinn introduced me to the writings of the mystics, most notably St. John of the Cross and St. Theresa of Avila. He also talked about St. Francis and his conversion from a life of drunken excess and lust to a conversion to a life of prayer and meditation. Father Abbot took a special interest in me; I believe he recognized my intelligence and my undeveloped spirituality. Several times he invited me to visit his special retreat nestled in the hills at the edge of Westcliffe. He encouraged me to continue my readings in philosophy. I now believe he was also a "Father" for me; a learned man who could guide me, in contrast to my own alcoholic father whose spirit was drowned in the "spirits" of drink.

Meanwhile I was visiting the Sheriff's office to ask for news for the Daily Record. The sheriff was a huge rather introverted man who shared his rodeo experiences. He was mainly a wild bull rider who said he had broken every bone in his body so badly he could no longer ride the beasts he loved. He had ridden in rodeos all over the West, but now had to accept those days were over.

Every year Cañon City had its own rodeo with a special prize for the girl they chose as Rodeo Queen. To win this distinction, the girls who were nominated had to pass a series of riding hurdles. The Sheriff proposed me as their candidate for Rodeo Queen; I would ride Snooks for this contest, a feat of trial and error. I felt honored to be chosen; it was the first rodeo I had attended. I prepared Snooks for this most important event by circling barrels and other skills a good horse and rider would possess. On rodeo day I was a bit apprehensive since the other contestants were western girls who grew up on ranches and who rode from the time they were children. But with the Sheriff's backing and the support of the firemen, the newspaper folks, and others who knew me through interviews, I rode forth to win the cherished prize and so celebrate the former bull rider. I rode into the ring, around the barrels, and flew through the other events, and was triumphantly on my way to home base. When all of a sudden my obstreperous Snooks headed fast for the exit and galloped out of the ring!!!

So the glory of Rodeo Queen was not to be mine, but all in attendance had a good laugh. You can imagine how hilarious the firemen chuckled and teased me about Snooks when I went for their news the next day.

Linda's Grammy: Linda, you have always been my pride and joy. I taught you how to read when you were only three. Then I introduced you to Thoreau and the transcendental writers. I told you about being a farm girl and my dream to see the Rocky Mountains. I picked you up from school and took you to a little park where you could be near the squirrels and trees. And I worried your father would hurt you when he broke down your bedroom door.

You were so bright and I hoped you would win a scholarship. I even went against my strict conscience and told you to smuggle home your sewing assignment so I could do it for you in case it kept you from a way to go to college. You were left handed and couldn't learn to manage a right handed machine.

And now you are living in the Rocky Mountains and invited me to visit! You even ran for Rodeo Queen. And most wonderful you ride Snooks through Phantom Canyon with a copy of Thoreau's *Walden* by your side.

I love you so much and I wish I could see you more.

Love, Grammy

CHAPTER 31

Snooks from Heavenly Pastures

Snooks: Hello, Linda, I'm so glad to see you. Do you have a carrot? I love that you let me live at a Benedictine Abbey, it was replenishing to my horsey soul.

I liked being with you, though I was sometimes hard to catch. I loved eating grass. And if I had a choice of being with you or eating grass—I chose grass every time. That's horse life. But you were good to me. I did want to be with you, too. We had many nice walks, and trots, and an occasional gallop. I owed you something. So I galloped. Sometimes.

I wanted to say I'm sorry if I galloped out of that inviting rodeo gate. I just felt we did really well, so well you might let me go home early. But I heard the crowd laughing as I left the arena with you. I knew I'd Horsed Up.

Anyway, I think of you fondly each day as I eat the heavenly clover here. I hope you think of me, too.

CHAPTER 32

And Away on Angel Wings You Flew

Keith: You loved Boulder and those Flatiron rocks, didn't you?

Linda: Boulder felt like Nirvana to me: at the foot of the mountains with the spectacular Flatiron rock formations at the bottom. Rock climbers came to climb them from everywhere, and some who fell to their deaths never returned home. The Mesa trail along their base stretched from its start at Chautauqua (home to festival goers in the summer and teachers in the school time) some eight miles to Eldorado Springs, a small hamlet with a natural mineral spring at its center. I hiked this trail many times and also rode Snooks there, too. Snooks was let loose in a pasture of horses where a rancher had placed an open railway car with hay for the horses in winter. If I wanted to ride him, I needed to catch him first. In his horsey world, Snooks reveled in freedom and made it hard for me to snag.

Keith: Ha, Snooks was a challenge, and you loved challenges. Tell me, how did you go from a Cañon City reporter to studying philosophy? That's a big jump.

Linda: Behind the Flatirons towered the eastern face of the Rocky Mountains covered with snow in winter and a haven for skiers like myself. Boulder also was home to University of Colorado, CU: the famous "play school" for fraternities as well as Nobel prize winners in the sciences. There I began studies for my master's degree in philosophy. At the time in the early sixties, women were discouraged from teaching careers in philosophy. When my master's thesis advisor learned that I was getting married he said, "That's a relief. Philosophy is no place for a woman."

Keith: Meaning only old men like him could make a living teaching philosophy. Ha!

Linda: He didn't know that my husband was encouraging me to pursue a doctorate in philosophy—a goal that had not been my own.

Keith: So you met a husband at CU? How did that go?

Linda: When I first saw my future husband across the cafeteria, I was immediately attracted. Ed was older, tall, and looked like an Englishman. With the help of a friend, I set about to meet him and learned that he was a physicist about to get his doctorate degree. Since he liked being a student, he prolonged his studies until he was one year from the deadline to finish his thesis. One of his thesis committee advisors was the famous Soviet physicist and cosmologist, George Gamow, world renowned for his contributions to the Big Bang theory, other physics theories, and who wrote the bestseller *One, Two, Three... Infinity*, a book I had read on the subway while commuting to Temple University. This huge, personable, vodka-swilling jokester was interested in the philosophy of science, but the other members of Ed's committee were not.

Ed was eccentric, an introvert who was nevertheless a charismatic teacher, and his deepest desire was to prove the existence of God through mathematics and physics, an aim that appealed to me.

Keith: That's a large ambition.

Linda: He was a philosopher of science and read my philosophy books with me. But he needed to finish his dissertation, so my ability to follow concepts and complete goals through to their finish enabled him to complete his thesis. And he encouraged me to get a doctorate in philosophy, a goal which had not been mine.

Keith: Like-minded philosophers, both of you. Yes. A good match.

Linda: So. We married in 1964 when I was twenty-four and he was thirty-three. He was gentle and kind and we had a creative life together. With Ed, I saw my first foreign film: an Ingmar Bergman double feature of *The Seventh Seal* and *The Virgin Spring*. I had never seen anything like them. Bergman depicted a realm for which I did not yet have a name. But I knew that his films showed a reality that I would be impelled to explore. Years later I understood that Bergman was tapping into an area that Jung would call the "collective unconscious." So the films pre-figured my next career to be a Jungian Analyst.

At that time, Phyllis Kenevan, a woman professor, came to CU to teach philosophy. Her classes were in existentialism and the philosophy of literature.

Keith: My goodness, two women into philosophy, what was the world coming to!

Linda: Coming to good things. She introduced us to Dostoyevsky, her beloved novelist. I audited the classes and discovered my true calling—to study the existential philosophers Heidegger, Jaspers, Unamuno, Marcel, Buber, Tillich, Dostoyevsky, and Camus—and then to inspire students as she had inspired me. I was too shy to approach her although she was friendly with students. But she was a muse and I admired her from afar.

Keith: She brought you one more step closer to your true self. Yes?

Linda: Yes. A decade later, when I was given a teaching job at the University of Colorado in Denver, I did meet Phyllis since her husband, Charlie, taught philosophy there. And we became good friends. No doubt this was a synchronicity that again changed the course of my life.

Keith: A miracle in a chance meeting… And your marriage with Ed? How did that fare?

Linda: Ed and I had a good marriage for that time. He was inspiring. Our life was to study together. We moved to Duquesne University in Pittsburgh where Ed taught physics and I studied for the doctorate. We had virtually no social life—a condition that eventually led to our separation. Neither of us drank alcohol so we did not have to contend with that dilemma. Our free time was devoted to watching foreign films which we loved. Studies at Duquesne, a Catholic university that hired philosophy professors from Europe, were stimulating and inspiring. The teachers were all writing books and applying the work of European writers to special subjects. Unlike those at CU, they were creative and wanted their students to be creative, too.

Keith: And the writing and creative work well suited you, I know.

Linda: Along with Ed I started to teach. My first job was to teach a class in Logic at a junior college in which the students were mostly boys who didn't want to learn. The boys were very rowdy and I couldn't control the class. And Logic was not a discipline I liked. I wanted to quit, but Ed told me he would come to my class to see if he could reach them.

Keith: That's a mark of good character, I think. Helping you.

Linda: Ed was very charismatic and told the students that if they didn't settle down and give me a chance to teach, the class would be canceled and they would be out of luck. He related to them in a non-dictatorial way; he was able to reach them in a way they understood. So they behaved and I was able to finish the semester.

Keith: You both won. Did you keep teaching?

Linda: Yes. Next I taught philosophy at a Catholic girls' college, Mount Mercy. Later the name was changed to Carlow College. The philosophy department and the college were very liberal. I could teach whatever I wanted. Hence I taught Nietzsche, Kierkegaard, Heidegger, and the other existential philosophers. I loved teaching and I loved the students, many of whom were nuns.

Keith: Courteous good students. Ha, I'm sure. So your life with Ed, it was fine, all stable?

Linda: Ah, no. I was also beginning to have a social life. I became friends with the art teacher to whom I became attracted. With him I took what I came to call my first real drink. We had agreed to meet for dinner. He offered me a glass of red wine. I hesitated because the film *Of Wine and Roses* flashed into my mind. In it, Jack Lemmon asks Lee Remick if she would like some wine. She accepts the wine which later becomes her downfall. Like her father, she becomes an alcoholic who cannot stop drinking, while Lemmon is a social drinker but not an alcoholic. He doesn't understand why she can't stop like he can. Although I had a warning from my memory I, too, took the drink. And like Remick's character, with it I began to fall into an abyss.

Keith: Things start, things end. I see it. Sorry.

Linda: They did end. And something new began for me. While at Duquesne I audited psychology classes. The psychology teachers would sit in on the philosophical studies. I read Ludwig Binswanger's book on Heidegger and psychopathology and loved it. I discovered Medard Boss's masterpiece, *Daseinsanalysis and Psychoanalysis.* Now I discovered I might like to be a psychotherapist—a career that was to become my third. I wrote to Boss who lived in Switzerland and asked if I could study with him. He asked me to send my dissertation on Heidegger and the notion of detachment. He liked it and offered to meet to explore studying with him. And so I went to Zurich, which would be my home for the next few years.

Keith: And away on angel wings you flew.

CHAPTER 33

Zurich, a First Journey into Myself

Linda: My trip to Zurich to meet Medard Boss heralded more than I could imagine. I fell in love with Zurich, the culture, the arts, opera, the historic cities of Europe. And as always hiking, skiing, and horseback riding in the Alps. I also began psychoanalysis.

Medard Boss was a warm, instinctual man and I had my first ever psychotherapy sessions with him. Despite his warmth, I froze; unaware of the tumultuous feelings held for thirty years within. Boss told me that while I could study with him, he could not give me a diploma since I did not have an M.D. However there was in Zurich a place that gave diplomas to students like myself called the C.G. Jung Institute and perhaps I could study there. So I went. When I met the director, Jim Hillman, he told me he didn't like Heidegger. But upstairs at that very moment Ludwig Binswanger's daughter was teaching; he took me to her class to see how I liked it. She was teaching a course on Demeter and Persephone about mothers and daughters, a subject directly related to me. I arranged to have a therapy session with her.

Hilde Binswanger was a very introverted woman with a brilliant subtle mind and warmth held within. She sat at a round table and on it were strange little objects like crystal balls and animal figurines. She asked me about my feelings; I found this disturbing and determined not to come for a second session. But that night I had the strangest dream, a nightmare that left me gasping. In it a woman with a masculine jacket was my mother who told me coldly that I was to care for her son, a young man who was developmentally disabled. She left and then I was in the dark galley of a large ship. I groped at a switch to turn on a light and saw two men hanging from the ceiling by their necks. One was alive and shouted for me to get him down; he was a baker and reminded me of Zorba the Greek. Then the other one fell to the ground; it was the "Young Man With a Lack" (emotional deprivation). Hysterically I grabbed a hose to beat him so he could not hurt me. The dream was so frightening it sent me back to Hilde Binswanger to understand it. And so began years of training to understand dreams and to become a Jungian Analyst.

Before I could study at the Jung Institute in Zurich I returned to the United States to keep my commitment as assistant professor of philosophy at San Diego State University. My husband went with me and took a year off to work on his project to prove the existence of God. I loved teaching and now added Jung to the readings. The students were older since I taught at night; after class we would go for drinks and continue philosophical talk.

My office mate, Alan Anderson, introduced me to the I Ching, the tarot, to astrology and other esoteric arts. I was lucky indeed to be blessed with deep thinkers at my side and a husband who encouraged my intellectual prowess.

But my heart remained in Zurich, with a huge transference to Hilde, my analyst, and I longed to return. I won a post-doctoral fellowship from the American Council of Learned Societies to research the relationship between Heidegger and Jung. With this grant, plus my savings, I now had the finances to study in Zurich. I asked my husband to join me, but he declined. I left for Zurich alone. Although we wrote letters, we never saw each other again; our lives drifted apart.

Keith: Dear Linda, oh that was a terrifying dream. It really shocked you. These two hanging men, did they represent recent fears, or family trauma arising? Where did they come from?

Linda: Oh, I discussed it deeply with Hilde Binswanger in our second meeting. "The Young Man with a Lack" represented my emotional deprivation. It sprung up initially from my becoming frozen in front of Boss, whom I was unprepared to share my feelings with. It involved my weakness due to the emotional deprivation that I long experienced in my family; I dissociated as a defense against my father's drinking. And then I realized the second man, who was a baker and shouted for me to cut him down—I realized this was about my Grandfather, who was a baker, a mean drunk whom

I feared, and who once drunkenly knocked over a stove, caused a threatening fire. These were deep wounds that had come right up inside me, and a first step to understanding my dreams and my inner self. And thus Jungian analysis broke open my world.

CHAPTER 34

Meeting A Dream Face to Face

Linda: While working with Hilde I had many dreams. A striking one involved a giant white swan. The huge enormous swan was pulling a raft and on it was a man. I wondered where it was going. Hilde's response was unexpected. She asked me if I had ever gone to an opera. I said "No." Then she told me an opera was playing that evening and suggested that I go.

Always eager to please her and try something new, I went to the opera that night. Wagner's opera, *Lohengrin*, was on. In it a giant swan pulls a raft towards the home of the Holy Grail. It is a romantic opera and part of the *Knight of the Swan* legend. My dream, with its image of the swan, and its role in Wagner's opera, is a classic example of the role of amplification in which a symbol is shown in both the dream and a legend that gives meaning to the dreamer. In my case it highlighted both romance and spiritual quest for meaning. The swan was also connected with my walks after analytical sessions along the lake where the elegant white birds swam.

CHAPTER 35

Zurich Wonderland

Keith: I think that Zurich let grow your inner grace. Is that right, you blossomed there? A red rose free to grow.

Linda: Oh, Keith, it was a wonderland—Zurich is a stunning city. The Limmat River runs through its medieval Old Town where it flows from Lake Zurich some 25 miles long. The twin towers of the Grossmunster Church and the Fraumunster Church, famous for its Chagall stained-glass windows, adorn each side of the Limmat and are surrounded by cobblestone streets, hidden alleys, and historic Guild houses. The narrow lanes on each side climb up steep hills and end at hiking trails that stretch high into the furthest reaches above the lake. On one side is the zoo and the cemetery where Thomas Mann and James Joyce are buried at the edge of the woods. *Wanderweges* (foot trails) stretch to the Greifensee lake where the devoted can hike and ride horses. The other side, at the summit of Uetliberg mountain, paths pass through valleys and forests; open air restaurants sit on high with panoramic views to the lake and the city of Zurich.

Keith: I wish we were there to walk it together right now.

Linda: Oh yes, there I found things I longed for! Zurich was home to artists and writers. Herman Hesse stayed at a sanatorium across the lake from Jung's house. *Steppenwolf*, Hesse's novel of a man split by despair, loneliness, and lack of belonging is set in the Niederdorf, the lower village, once home to prostitutes, thieves and other outsiders. His novel, *Demian*, a depiction of the characters encountered in the psyche, was written after Hesse underwent analysis by a Jungian psychiatrist. The Dadaist artists lived in Zurich as did Albert Einstein and many Nobel prize winners. I felt surrounded by good company.

Along the Zurich Lake, a walkway extends until it reaches the Fischstube, one of many renowned gourmet restaurants. Elegant white swans, parading their long graceful necks, swim in the lake along with ducks and other water creatures. Jung's home and grave is in Kusnacht beside the lake, and the tower he built by hand lies in Bollingen at its end.

Keith: So you were spiritually and philosophically home. And you felt welcome, Dear Linda.

CHAPTER 36

My Transference: I Was Totally In Love With Him

Linda: Training in Zurich was deep and manifold. Personal analysis was the keystone. I went for sessions four days a week and my life was devoted to plumbing the depths. Most of us were on "Night Sea Journeys," the archetypal quest to descend into the unconscious in search of understanding, and to discover that which was hidden in ourselves, so that we could return transformed.

Keith, on seeing a picture of me taken while I was walking by the Zurich Lake after an analytical session, you said, "Linda, you look so depressed you must have been on a trip through Hell." And Hell it was indeed. I had to look at all the emotions, thoughts and actions that had been repressed due to my traumatic childhood, my shame, and anger that had been submerged.

I was reminded of my dream in a boat going through an underworld cavern in which dragons and crocodiles were chained to the walls. The chains were important because they allowed me to look at monsters in myself without being devoured by them. The boatman said, "We will come out from Hades, from this realm of the dead. But to undertake this mission we must be able to see that which is hidden so we can identify the dangerous parts of ourselves, in order to transform them into characters of creativity."

While trainees were undergoing the journey that was unique to them, they were also studying the works of Jung, along with myths of different cultures and religions that held meaning for their metamorphosis and renewal. International scholars came to the Jung Institute to give profound insights in their fields. Heinrich Zimmer shared his research on the symbols and art of Indian philology. Giles Quispel, historian and theologian of Christianity and Gnosticism, spoke about his studies of religion. Laurens van der Post lectured on the Bushmen of the Kalihari in Africa.

As trainees, we also learned how to interpret fairy tales; Marie Louise von Franz, an expert in the field, maintained that understanding fairy tales was the best way to gain insight and analyze dreams.

After attending a semester of study, we were interviewed by members of the Curatorium, the governing body of the Institute. Because of my studies with Medard Boss and my background in Heidegger, I was considered suspect by some, since Boss focused on Heidegger and Freud as important to the art of therapy, and in this way departed from Jung. I learned that I needed to keep a low profile.

Then we were given exams in a variety of studies: dream interpretation, fairy tales and mythology, history of psychoanalysis, psychopathology, world religions, and the works of Jung. I was lucky at the dream exam. Jolanda

Jacobi, an early Jungian scholar, asked me to give an example of a dream and how understanding it helped transform the dreamer. Immediately I thought of Dostoyevsky's character, Raskolnikov, in *Crime and Punishment* and related the dream he had which showed he was not above morality, but had compassion, and therefore was capable of redemption. Frau Dr. Jacobi was so impressed that I passed all the exams with ease. My background in literature and philosophy also made the theoretical exams easy to do.

Once through this initial hurdle, we were allowed to take clients under supervision. Before graduating, we had to take another series of tests, write a thesis, and visit psychiatric clinics. There clinic patients were brought out and a psychiatrist would explain their malady and diagnosis. Most notable of these were patients from Sanitorium Bellevue, situated at the lake of Constance separating Germany from Switzerland.

Bellevue was known all over Europe and was different because the Binswanger family, who managed the hospital, believed that the patients would heal better without the typical hierarchy of doctor to patient. Bellevue doctors did not wear white coats and the patients, whenever possible, were allowed to live in houses and to walk around the grounds freely. Bellevue became home for intellectuals and artists since its emphasis on creativity allowed them to be themselves. Nijinsky, the Russian ballet dancer, performed his extraordinary "Dance of Death" while a patient in Bellevue—a performance that Hilde, who grew up there, saw as a child. In wartime, Kirchner painted his expressionist art there in peace.

During the Nazi period Hilde's mother, who was German, helped refugees cross from the German side of the lake to freedom in Switzerland. Hilde's father, Ludwig Binswanger, founded the field of existential analysis, a synthesis of psychoanalysis and existential philosophy, and wrote his masterpiece book, *Being-in-the-World*, there.

As my supervisors for client therapy, I chose Jung's grandson, Dieter Baumann, and the brilliant author, Guggenbuhl-Craig. And third, my new additional analyst, Helmut Barz M.D., I chose as well. All candidates were advised to be analyzed by both a man and a woman to develop both masculine and feminine sides.

As I analyzed with Barz, I developed a new overwhelming transference; I was totally in love with him.

Linda viewing the Duino Castle.

CHAPTER 37

Journeys to Find the Self

Linda: Helmut Barz was German and a highly cultured literate man. He later became president of the Zurich Jung Institute. I first encountered him when he taught a course in psychopathology based on the book by the existential psychiatrist Karl Jaspers.

Rilke was his favorite poet and mine, too. Barz encouraged me to undertake a series of pilgrimages to Duino Castle above Trieste, Italy, where Rilke captured the first poem of the *Elegies*, and to his grave in Raron, Switzerland, where he finished the *Elegies* and then wrote the twenty-two sonnets of *The Sonnets to Orpheus*. Later, inspired by him, I wrote my thesis, "Rilke and the Poetry of the Self."

Barz also sent me to visit his mother in Hamburg and from there I travelled to Lubeck to see the sculpture of Ernst Barlach. I mention these trips because they were the most influential part of my training as an analyst. Unlike all other Jung Institutes, Zurich exposed its students directly to European culture, which became central to understanding the human condition, an indispensable part of an analyst's work which exceeds the purely personal and includes world knowledge—the awareness of the collective unconscious.

My first therapist, Hilde, had also fostered my love of travel; I explored the Romantische Strasse to see the alters of Tilman Riemenschneider; I went to Norway where I fell in love with the paintings of Edvard Munch.

Keith, you have asked me to describe my travels since they show an important part of who I am. I went to the great cities of Europe—Paris, Vienna, Amsterdam. But it was to Berlin that I was drawn. The Berlin Wall cordoned off east from west; it was Cold War times. In the west the Wall had regard neither for Nature nor human life; it cut through rivers interrupting their flow, split woods apart and ruptured meadows. Worse yet it divided people. Since I was from German grandparents I tried to track my name. Yes, there were two families with Schierse as a last name but they were in East Berlin. I tried to call but it was impossible; human communication was severed.

Despite the Wall, museums were also on the west side. I discovered the art of Kathe Kollwitz whom I admire to this very day. She lived and worked with the poor people of Berlin, painting the suffering in their faces. A street and a park are named in her honor today.

Another of my trips was to visit my existential philosopher, Heidegger. With a friend we travelled to Freiburg, took some flowers and found his house. A knock brought his wife to the entry; she was a housefrau who said we were not welcome and closed the door in our face. We didn't allow this to discourage us since we knew he had a hut in the Schwarzwald. We drove there to Todnauberg (Death Mountain) and went straight to the pub to learn where he might live. The pub owner laughed and pointed to a slope above the hamlet. "Heidegger keeps his hut open for anyone to enter. He has placed his hut up highest, but still below the tree line, in order not to be above the divinities. He comes to the pub often to be with the locals."

We hiked up the steep hill and entered the cabin; it was small but had a stove, a table, and a cot. A small journal lay on a stove with handwritten notes. I was sure this must be part of an original work he was still writing. I tried to decipher the text with my limited German. Yes, one word is fire and another wood. He must be writing poetically about these beauties! I struggled along with my translation. When I was finished I read what I wrote: I had uncovered not a major work, but rather directions on how to light a fire in the stove.

So Keith, do laugh, the "Fool" here is not you, but me.

CHAPTER 38

For Madmen Only

Linda: During a session, Helmet Barz said he could imagine me as a young girl sitting by an upstairs window and playing the violin—a romantic image I loved. With Helmut I became seductive, wearing clothes that showed my figure.

He once described me as his "dark anima"—an archetypal feminine character that I proceeded to act out. I went to a night club in the Niederdorf—the bohemian area in Zurich where the prostitutes hang out and the very street where Hesse's *Steppenwolf* found the "Magic Theater," where its entrance said "For Madmen Only." A fellow student, who was seeking admittance to the Jung Institute, took me there to sample a blend of drugs and marijuana—some kind of weed that I had never tried. It may have been hashish laced with Angel dust. As soon as we smoked it, the student insulted me, started a negative criticism of me that had to do with Heidegger, thus fostering a negative reaction that turned into a living nightmare. I didn't know this guy very well and I didn't know why he wanted to scare me. He became "the tall thin man in black"—a frightening figure from childhood dreams. Now delusional, I thought he was trying to trick me into jumping into the Limmat river where I would drown. The next several hours I spent trying to get away from him. He scared me by saying that the trains and the trams stopped at midnight; I would not be able to return to my analysts' housing. I was lost and confused even though my apartment was only a twenty-minute walk up the hill. After some hours I found a friend's place. She told me to come inside and told him to go away. Then she told me to sit down and start translating a book in German. This activity cleared my head and grounded me.

I told Helmut about this event. The student was not accepted into training. But Helmut went to this weed club himself to see what other shadows lurked in the night. He was clearly intrigued. However, Helmut invited me to have lunch at his house where I would meet his wife and children. Later I realized he hoped this would present me with the reality of his life outside the therapy room. It took a long time for me to get over my transference. But eventually I did, and on visits back to Zurich years later, we met for dinner in a normal way.

CHAPTER 39

Leaving Paradise

Linda: I had to return home to teach. My money ran out. Earlier the Institute gave me a scholarship and half-loan along with my commitment to see clients from its clinic. But that period was over; I had completed my studies except for my thesis, which I could write anywhere. My job teaching at San Diego State University was open. I went back although I longed to stay and live in Zurich.

In 1973 I chose to teach a semester at Sonoma State University. If I had to work in the United States, I wanted to live in San Francisco. While in Zurich I was befriended by Marjorie and Gordon Foster, who told me that Mill Valley, where they lived, was beautiful and cultural. Sonoma State was only a hour away. I also went back into therapy with their friend, Ludwig Lefevbre, who translated the works of Karl Jaspers and was an existential psychoanalyst. He was fatherly and thought my major obstacle to finding a good relationship was repressed anger. He was right.

Grammy and Linda posing with Snooks.

CHAPTER 40

Death by Fire

One evening my phone rang. Friends of my mother called to tell me that my father had burned down the house. My grandmother was killed in the fire. The house was black and charred. My father had been smoking and drinking. He passed out and his cigarette fell to the couch which set it afire. My grandmother was upstairs and trapped. Although my father awoke and tried to get to her, it was too late. She was ninety-six and still with a good mind.

I caught the first plane to Philadelphia to be with my mother who had been at work at the time.

I don't know how my mother dealt with this tragedy. But she was a survivor. We cried many times together.

I spoke to my grandmother now in a casket. I read passages from the *Tibetan Book of the Dead.* My beloved grandmother, Grammy, was gone from the earthly plane. She was the one who believed in me. She nurtured me and taught me to read, write, and study. She shared her fantasy of seeing the Rocky Mountains—a dream that I was able to fulfill when my mother drove me to Cañon City. I thanked her again as she lay lifeless in a coffin. I wished I had visited her more. Oh how I loved her! She knew that, but I wished in my heart I had told her more often.

What an irony that Grammy died in the fire. When I was a child, she always had worried that I might be trapped in a fire accidentally set by my father. So I was never left alone at home to avoid this dreadful event. Now it was Grammy that died in the fire and not me. What a sad reversal of fates.

* * *

A few months later I had a consoling vision. In the dream Grammy was living in a lovely San Francisco apartment in Pacific Heights; she was happy that she could look out over the city even to see the bay below. She wore a blue dress and in her apartment blue was the dominant tone. Blue was her favorite color. The dream reassured me that Grammy had found her true place in heaven. Thank God I believed in dreams.

CHAPTER 41

The Inter-Regional Society of Jungian Analysts!

Linda: Keith, you asked me to explain how my careers intermeshed. Teaching at Sonoma State ended after spring semester 1973. I had been hired to replace a professor on sabbatical leave. I tried to find a job in San Francisco but failed. Then a surprise offer to teach at University of Colorado at Denver came my way. I accepted. Now I could return to Boulder, a paradise in my twenties.

Another career surprise came soon after. A new type of training institute for Jungian analysts was envisioned, the *Inter-Regional Society of Jungian Analysts*—one that could take applicants from all over the country. I was asked to join to take part in the planning.

Keith: Linda, what was the thought behind that, to create a "little Zurich"? So people unlike you wouldn't have to make your courageous journey to Switzerland by yourself, learn yourself deeply, and complete time honored study to be an authentic analyst? Was it a shortcut to becoming an analyst?

Without benefit of your striving, your goals? Or worse maybe just to make money in America?

Linda: No. Training in Zurich was difficult because it required money to live there; Switzerland had rules about jobs. A foreigner could work only if no Swiss person could perform the task. And those with a family had to separate for long periods of time. I was able to train there only because I won a post-doctoral fellowship and I had no children.

To answer your question about making money—wealth was not a major factor for those called to be analysts. Like yourself, healing oneself and others to become whole and creative is the aim.

The Zurich Institute was the first training center, but three others existed—those in New York, Los Angeles and San Francisco. *Inter-Regional* catered to isolated analysts like myself in Denver and provided a community.

Keith: Knowing what I do about psychiatrists and doctors, some of whom become self-serving stallions who boss their herds, how did you become involved with this group? Were there personalities that lent themselves to a new group vision? Did you feel comfortable? Were they using you in some way, or were things mutually beneficial?

Linda: I was called by other colleagues to help form this controversial training institute. Founding the schooling, mentoring the candidates, and working with colleagues enabled me to grow and to put muscle and flesh on my slender frame.

Seven analysts living in isolated areas came together to discuss the logistics. Three of us were new "green" analysts fresh out of Zurich—Murray Stein, Tom Kapacinkas, and myself. Two seasoned analysts spearheaded the venture: June Singer and James Hall. Bill Willeford from Seattle and Arwind Vasavada, an Indian analyst from Chicago, joined, too. The seasoned analyst who made the vision possible was Joe Wheelwright from San Francisco; Joe was known for his huge heart and ability to make things happen. Werner Engel from New York also helped.

Inter-Regional was intended to be temporary—an "umbrella" institute that would enable early candidates to become analysts. When they finished the "umbrella" would close. I never liked this idea. I could see the Inter-Regional Jungian Institute become a lasting force.

Keith: So it was for a select few, and they would do the selecting. And once they did their selection, the association would close? Strange. I understand how you wouldn't agree with that. What were the first meetings like, done in dark rooms with candles? Or was it more open?

Linda: We first met at an airport hotel in Saint Louis. We put forward our ideas for training. We both loved and fought in this process. Two opposing groups emerged: one emphasizing practical concerns for licensing; the other arguing for emphasis in the humanities. I was a rebel and for the humanities, along with Tom Kap, Bill Willeford, and Vasavada (who was said to have a begging bowl rather than regular fees in his practice).

Keith: And what specifically did you want the humanities side to include? And tell me more about what licensing meant? How would they do that?

Linda: As a student of literature and film, I knew how important the humanities were to understand the complexity and paradoxes of the human condition. I saw being a Jungian analyst as an "art" rather than a methodical science.

The practical problem of getting a license to practice was not addressed in Zurich. In the United States, each individual state had its own rules to meet requirements. Translating European education into American terms was difficult. Eventually I was required to apply my more esoteric studies to California's rigorous standards in order to obtain a license there. Remember this was over half a century ago. Jung was regarded with suspicion by scientists in the field.

This division between licensing and humanities lasted for years on end. At one meeting Joe Wheelwright and Jeff Raff fought so hard that they had to be separated.

Keith: How did you all get together, did you choose a home base, Denver or somewhere?

Linda: We met twice a year in different cities where we gave intensive training. Maybe we were a bit like a traveling circus. Of course we had to contend with the "shadow" side of each other. But this was an important part of each analyst's growth. For example, June Singer and I were uncomfortable shadow figures for each other. But as we grew, we learned to appreciate the strengths of the other. June was strong in practical thinking. She also had a marvelous gift for aesthetics and detail. I was intuitive, open, and loose at the time; I wrote out of chaos; she wrote out of form. Eventually we came to respect and honor each other—a gift of grace that I value today. Keith, I remember in Prague when we spent time with June and went to the synagogue that displayed paintings of children from the concentration camp or Terezin, you went over to her and shared her sensitivity and suffering. June never forgot your incredible empathy and understanding; in that moment you were her healer. You had that rare gift of tender insight and compassion that was so healing for me and others you met.

Keith: So you came together, settled differences, and then made calls to find scholars interested in studying with you?

Linda: No, we did not seek other scholars. Rather analysts and candidates sought us out to join. We started by having a set of interviews for applicants. All of us were on every committee unless one of our own candidates was on trial. We worked hard by day. We played hard at night. Drinking and dancing to let off steam.

The trainings were held in different places—one in the spring and the other in autumn. Soon we were deluged by more and more applicants from all over the states, Canada, Mexico, and Latin America. Inter-Regional was growing. The "umbrella" idea was dropped. The institute which first began in 1973 exists today, over half a century old.

Keith: So success, and then comes transferences, complicating relations. Did that happen much?

Linda: Yes, transferences and crossed boundaries occurred and, of course, we had to deal with difficult situations. My own transgressions were due to drinking. I had blackouts that prevented me from accurate memory. Later, when I went into recovery, I learned how to make amends.

Keith: Linda, did you find being part of Inter-Regional a good experience, so different from Zurich?

Linda: I learned about conflict in our early meetings. It was my first "group" experience. Now I could present my own perspective. I could also back down when I saw another's truth. Since I had no siblings, I did not have to deal with wishes of others. It was my mother, Grammy, and me against my Dad. Thus I was shy and didn't like to argue. Instead I would withdraw. Training in Zurich focused upon the individual. Groups were taboo in the early days. But Inter-Regional emphasized cooperation. My "softness" was made stronger and sturdy. My "*Puella*" self became integrated with the "*Amazon.*"

Young Linda with her Father.

CHAPTER 42

My Father Dies, *The Wounded Woman* Born

My father died in 1975 from a heart attack brought on by years of drinking. He never acknowledged that he was an alcoholic. I knew I had to reconcile with him somehow. I spent years hating him for traumatizing my childhood, for making my mother's life so hard, and for the fire which killed my grandmother. I decided to write about my father's syndrome, about the "*wounded father.*"

Most people are unaware of the terrible conditions that plague the family of an alcoholic.

Most nights were frightening, never knowing when and how my father would be when he came home. Usually he arrived around three a.m. after the bars closed at two a.m. He made a lot of noise and wakened neighbors. Inside he would talk in different accents that drove me crazy. Even though he might have been in a good mood, my mother was angry and tore into him. Then he became threatening, even violent toward my grandmother. One time he pushed her down the steps, a fall that hurt her. I also remember him having a knife in his hands, but have repressed the reason why. A fight would ensue, and when my mother tried to get to the phone, he would block the way. In terror I had to run outside to call for help, hoping a neighbor would call the police. One time when the police came, they told my mother that she had to sign him into a psychiatric ward because the calls were too frequent. I remember crying on the couch and a kind policeman saying to my father: "How can you do this to your daughter?"

Some nights my father tried to get into my bedroom; he complained that my mother didn't want to be sexual with him and wanted to tell me about his frustration. If I had my bedroom door closed and locked, he knocked it down to get inside. This caused a general hysteria. I had an adjoining door with my grandmother and went to her for comfort. But my mother was now enraged and so a violent fight ensued. These incidents were frequent. He also threatened to phone my beloved Aunt Sally who had a heart condition. He knew this would scare us and made these attempts often. Later my analyst, Don Sandner, would say: "The problem is your father in the bedroom doorway."

I was always afraid he might follow me to school. Hiding this from the neighbors was impossible. But school was far enough away from home that I could hide my shame through my good grades. Shame, shame, shame! The life of the child of an alcoholic.

My father was also thrown into jail many times for being drunk and disorderly. One night a hospital aide called my mother. My father had been run over by a trolley. He was often beaten up and robbed by mean men who took out their own abuse on him.

When my father was put inside the psychiatric ward of Philadelphia General Hospital, my mother forced me to go with her to see him even though I was underage. I hated it there and remember a foul smell of coffee that frightens me still to this day, a sign of PTSD that can last a lifetime. When we reached his ward, I saw he had no belt to hold up his pants. He was humiliated there and not treated properly. He was given electric shock treatments that broke his ribs! In those days alcoholism was not considered to be a disease.

Another time, before his disease totally consumed him and he was still able to work, he came home with a lot of money. As a settlement clerk, he had helped the sale of a famed hotel in Atlantic City, one that is named on Monopoly boards. He threw the money at my mother and left. Soon after bags of gourmet groceries arrived along with a television. My father disappeared for two years. I prayed to God that he wouldn't return. But eventually he came back to our dismay.

I still don't understand why my mother forced me to go with her to see him in this degraded condition. Did she want me to share her own mortified disgrace?

After my describing these horrors of my father, it might seem that he was a weak-willed bad person. Actually, I think he was an intelligent sensitive man, who suffered from a dreaded disease, and whose father was also an alcoholic. But the repressed feelings of shame still haunt me today and so I must write about them.

* * *

Jung emphasizes the importance of synchronicity—the outer event which coincides with inner meaning and which are not causally related. Not surprising, then, that at this very moment of my father's death, a colleague asked me to give a lecture in the city where she lived. My teaching job at University of Colorado, Denver allowed me to pick my own reading list. I decided to include books that described some patterns I had found to be at fault in the development of women, patterns that I could present at the lecture. And so I began writing for a book that would later become *The Wounded Woman.*

I became a cafe writer in the tradition of Sartre and Simone de Beauvoir. At lunchtime around two p.m. I headed for a bistro, ordered a meal and wine, and would write for three to four hours.

Then I would stop writing, but order more wine. I grew into a "drinking writer," a romantic ideal from my European days. My writing and teaching augmented each other while my work as an analyst gave depth to my understanding of human life. As I lectured more on this topic, I realized that other women had difficulties with their fathers, though much different than my own. What began as a lecture and article expanded into a book length study the longer I read and wrote.

I saw two opposing patterns of women emerge: the "*Puella*," or girl, and the "*Armored Amazon*," the aggressive woman. These patterns were akin to Hillman's opposing *puer* and *senex* within the masculine field. But so far no one had written about the female forms, nor about the father-daughter relationship. I called my first article "The Puer's Daughter" and the second "The Armored Amazon." My view was that these opposing patterns both existed in women. The challenge would be to integrate them into a creative mode.

Writing *The Wounded Woman* from start to publication took seven years. I began in 1975 and was given the finalized printed copy in 1982. I first submitted it to publishers in 1980 and received 42 rejections. A few female editors said they liked the book, but their marketing department didn't think it would sell. An editor at one of the top publishing houses kindly gave me the reports of the readers to whom it was sent. The readers were women with graduate degrees in psychology. All had the same criticism. I had put my own heart and soul on the line and shared my personal experience along with my analytical discussion of the father-daughter wound. The readers thought personal experience should not be included by a professional psychologist; their advice was to delete my private ordeals so my discourse could be empirically objective.

I could not accept this suggestion. It would destroy the fruits of my labor. I had written *The Wounded Woman* to share my personal story with my readers so they would feel they were not alone and cut off from a professional healer. We were all together affected by the *father wound.* Sharing my story was essential to healing the hurt and pain of the trauma. It included men as well as women—the fathers were wounded, too.

Now, half a century later, it is common for psychologists to be frank and honest about their own suffering. But fifty years earlier this was taboo.

I was determined to follow my heart and gut instinct and to continue to search for a publisher. If I felt something strongly, I rarely abandoned my goal. And the years I spent listening to women, whose lives were impacted by their wounded fathers, were a testament to my commitment to try to heal the insulted and injured souls.

At a lecture in Chicago, Murray Stein introduced me and said that he hoped there might be in the audience a publisher who would see the value of my book. He was right. After the lecture was over, an editor from Swallow Press, Donna Ippolito, approached me, saying she would like to read my manuscript, and if she liked it, she would buy it without demanding radical changes. But she added that she would also give me suggestions to make it better—recommendations that I could accept or deny.

I was thrilled. Swallow was a fine literary press that published Anais Nin's journals and Frank Waters' Pueblo Indian mythology, and Donna Ippolito had edited their masterful works. I awaited her review. She liked my book, but sent me ten single-space pages of suggestions. I followed them and with her created a stronger book. She sent my book to the poet May Sarton who received it on her seventieth birthday. Sarton liked *The Wounded Woman* since it caused her to rethink her own relationship with her father, and she gave the book an outstanding recommendation—a blurb that would enhance the back cover. In addition, the writer who wrote for the San Francisco Chronicle reviewed my book and two other more academic tomes on the same subject and gave mine an outstanding rating. That suddenly three books on the father-daughter relationship were released suggested to me that an archetype had sprung forth on this new topic. In the meantime Ohio University Press bought Swallow and became the official publisher. They sold the paperback rights to Shambhala who enhanced the book with a beautiful cover—and suddenly my book became a best seller and remained there for eight months. Eventually it was translated into twenty languages and became an international success.

CHAPTER 43

The Wounding. The Hurting. The Healing.

Jean: Ah, good morning, Linda. It's so kind of you to come and visit your neighbor, old Jean Le Fou. I have something to confess to you—you changed my life.

Linda: Oh, how so, Jean? Of course, my standard fee for analysis will apply to this confession.

Jean (laughing): Ah, Linda, you are so cruel in your humor. But always in a loving way. I want to confess to you that I read your book, *The Wounded Woman*, when I was thirty-five, some forty years ago. It transformed my life. Saved me really. I've always wondered how you came to write such an amazing work.

Linda: *The Wounded Woman* combined my three careers—teaching, Jungian analysis, and writing. I had been given the gift of seeing universal patterns of psychology, emotion, and behavior. So in talking with women I found two opposing archetypal motifs in their psyche: the "*Puella*" and the "*Armored Amazon*."

Women who lived out the *Puella*, the Latin word for girl, tended to be sensitive and vulnerable, often seen as charming but weak; underneath lay power that needed to be developed and nurtured in their lives. Their strength was often concealed in the "*Shadow,*" Jung's term for the undeveloped part of a person that lay hidden away from consciousness.

In contrast, the *"Armored Amazon"* showed force that frequently frightened others; but beneath a tremendous vulnerability was concealed that rendered her helpless in mature relationships. In Greek mythology the Amazon was a fierce woman warrior who instilled terror in those she fought.

Jean: And that's my confession, that your book was about women, but when I read it I found myself described there. I was a man, and yet I lived as a *Puella*. It led to a transformation of my life.

Linda: Jean, what type of *Puella*? May I ask?

Jean: Oh, it's so long ago, I don't recall exactly. Can you remind me? I remember being transformed.

Linda: Transformation requires identifying whatever is to be achieved. As I worked on it, I continued to dig further into people's stories and in the literature that I read. As I talked more with different types of women and read more in biographies, I delineated four subgroups in each category.

Jean, here is a list of the *Puella* and *Armored Amazon* types, did you fit any of these?

Jean (reading the list he's handed by Linda):

———

The Darling Doll**:** Adapts to the fantasy of her partner instead of developing who she wants and needs to be. Ibsen had written about this type of woman in his play "The Doll House." Her challenge is to recognize her dependence and to begin to live life on her own terms. This takes strength and qualities of the Amazon woman who can fight for her own rights to be respected for who she is.

The Girl of Glass**:** This *Puella* is often shy and fragile like the character in Tennessee Williams' *The Glass Menagerie.* She often lacks confidence and lives in her imagination. Her challenge is to step into the outer world and to actualize the images that are a source of creativity just as William's Laura surrenders her glass unicorn for a real horse.

The High Flyer: A *Puella* that likes to be as free as the wind and live in the world of possibilities seeking the world of adventure, risk, and danger. Anais Nin has described this mode of existence in her novel, *A Spy in the House of Life.* The challenge for the *High Flyer* is to recognize life's limits and boundaries and to commit to something concrete. Nin, who was a *High Flyer*, transformed herself through her writing.

The Misfit: A *Puella* who feels rejected, tends to rebel against parents or society. Sometimes these feelings are due to low self-esteem and shame that may come from having an addictive parent. Or she may be rebelling against a tyrannical authoritarian father. Arthur Miller described *The Misfit* in his play *After the Fall*, which he modeled on his wife, Marilyn

Monroe. She starred in the movie version called *The Misfits*. The way of redemption is to fight against feelings of shame, cynicism, or being a victim and to step forward bringing them out of the *Shadow* into creative life.

In contrast, the *Armored Amazon* shows her power in the world. But often this show of strength obscures the vulnerability that lies within.

The Super Star: Often compensating for a weak father, she works hard to be admired. But acclaim is a poor substitute for love. Sylvia Plath describes this phenomenon in her novel *The Bell Jar.* Overcompensation through work can be healed through an openness to playing like a child who needs no armor to be herself.

The Dutiful Daughter: She is bound to a strict discipline that is not her own but is demanded by an authoritarian figure. Simone de Beauvoir has described this mode of being. The challenge for the *Dutiful Daughter* is to surrender control in order to be open for the flow of life which involves dark sides like a river with black stones and soil beneath.

The Martyr: With her long suffering face, this *Armored Amazon* lives with self-denial that is a feature of having grown up in a loveless home. *The Martyr* is portrayed in Fellini's *Juliet of the Spirits*. Alexander Löwen has described this pattern in his book *Love and Orgasm*. The masochistic aspect of *The Martyr* may conceal a hidden sense of superiority. The challenge for *The Martyr* is to let go of her addiction to control and allow the surge of Dionysian life to carry her to creativity.

The Warrior Queen: A strong and determined fighter, she tends to oppose irrationality. C. S. Lewis has described her in his novel *Till We Have Faces.* This fighter's life can become a chore and a series of battles to be won rather than moments to be enjoyed. A challenge for her is to opt for receptivity, spontaneity, and openness for relationship.

Jean (looking up): Linda, I was mainly a *Puella*, the *Girl of Glass*, living in my imagination, but also a bit of the *Martyr*, with a hidden sense of superiority. I can describe my family as distant, nearly loveless.

Linda: And what transformed you?

Jean: Your book told me two things that I knew were true of me.

It said that I lived *without history*. And I thought… And it was true. If you asked me what I did on Wednesday last week, I couldn't tell you. I lived in a kind of timeless being. If you asked me who I was, I would give a vague answer, say I was, "a teacher." I didn't say my history—that I had two degrees, I lived five years overseas in Morocco and Algeria, I wrote poetry constantly. Instead I said, "I'm a teacher." I didn't carry my history with me, nor share it. And what your book said was true. I lived without history.

And the next thing it said to me, "This person lives in unconscious despair."

And I thought, "What?"

For me, despair was feeling sad, and I didn't feel sad. What did that mean? Unconscious despair? A despair I didn't know about? And I realized when I thought about the world, it was unhappy, out of touch, it was a moaning train horn calling through the night. I realized despair wasn't a feeling, it was my way of seeing the world. And as I looked around, despair was all around me.

My family had taught me as a child there was a God. But he never did the right thing, was neglectful, distance, uncaring. The world could be hurt and he walk right by. I could be good, deserve better, but nothing came to me, still alone. I had a God, a distant Lutheran God, who didn't do the right thing. I grew up expecting nothing from him. No answers.

And I thought, "No! This God is not good for me." And I quit believing, turned to believing in a different world. One where, yes, it was dangerous, you could be run over by a car, but, if you looked, it was also beautiful, there were things to care about, be lucky, achieve. And that's the world I chose to believe in.

And that's the moment my world transformed. I was free, free to be and do what I needed, to care, to love, to find the good. For the time I had.

And then, I cried. I cried feeling sorry for myself. Having this realization at thirty-five, when someone wiser might have told me this at fifteen. Saved me all those years wasted in despair. My tears. Solely for myself.

Then I was free, I did new things, I could be a fool and lucky. I changed my job, I made ten phone calls and sold an entire magazine company. In two weeks, the publisher had to pay me a year's salary for making just ten phone calls. My life changed for the good. I was lucky!

And from then on, I had a whole new journey of learning about myself.

Jean (getting on his knees): And so, Linda, I take your hand here and say thank you. Your book transformed my world, life. And it was a gift from you. And for the many thousands who had their lives changed by reading *The Wounded Woman*, we all thank you. And now I, forty years later thank you, too.

Linda smiles, says nothing.

Jean: So now, Linda, let me draw a card for us. As I always do. Just one card and we'll see our lives in it.

The Emperor!

The Emperor is the ruler of the kingdom. He is like a door through which all things come into his realm, and he is a window through which he sees the outer kingdom. The Emperor is the one who rules all that comes in and all that goes out of the kingdom.

And here is the secret. If your Emperor is fearful, angry, without love, all in the kingdom will be his prisoners. But if your Emperor is caring, kind, loving, discerning, joy will come into the kingdom. All the prisoners will go free.

And, Linda, thank you. You changed my Emperor to see clearly, with care, beauty, love, and—even miracles.

CHAPTER 44

Linda's Reply to Jean

From: Linda Schierse Leonard
To: jeanlefou@aol.com
Subject: Don't worry no charge

Hello Jean,

I won't be charging you for your confession today. So rest easy. (Ha.)

When you thanked me, I didn't know what to say. I felt blessed.

But I want to explain just a few things to you about the book's success. Many many women wrote me to say I had changed their lives. It was an honor to receive these letters.

The Wounded Woman was successful because it helped people become conscious of the role of the father in their lives. And it identified patterns that women lived out.

And the book included a description of the fathers themselves, extending beyond my own weak alcoholic father. Some fathers were tyrannical and authoritarian, holding their daughters to rigid standards of perfection that were not achievable.

Other fathers abandoned their daughters by ignoring their needs or by leaving them either through affairs, divorce, or disappearing geographically. Still others sexually abused their daughters leaving them with terrible traumas and PTSD syndromes to endure. The patriarchal society that devalued women's unique contribution was a major collective wound that dominated people's lives, keeping them prisoners like birds in a cage.

And then I received letters of thanks from fathers!

Fathers themselves wrote because I had written about their plight understanding that they themselves were wounded.

And this, beyond question, was an unexpected gift come to me. Whose father was, well, we've talked about it. You know that pain.

Have a good day for us both. Draw a card with a high number of Cups! Ha.

❤ Love,

Linda

CHAPTER 45

Hitting Bottom: A Taste of Bliss

When writing *The Wounded Woman* I had a secret wish. I hoped that by transforming the father complex I would be able to drink like a normal person. In the beginning Dionysian freedom brought ecstasy—a high that eluded me in ordinary life.

Before I went to Zurich I rarely drank alcohol. Neither my husband, Ed, nor I drank. Our life of study and work didn't permit excess.

In Europe, it was common to drink wine with meals both at lunch and dinner. And so I began to enjoy wine when I ate and appreciated gourmet fare accompanied by a glass of Fendant, a fine white wine from Swiss vineyards. Soon this became a customary pleasure in my way of life. Social life became easier for me, in contrast to the anxiety that I felt at group gatherings. On hikes in the countryside, I saw outdoor restaurants pop up every few kilometers, offering a place to sit and enjoy nature along with a delicious glass of vino. I especially liked to walk through vineyards to enjoy their colorful beauty along with the thought that a tasting might ensue.

Soon I noticed a pleasing high whenever I drank spirits—and even a special euphoria.

But what began as a natural complement to meals soon became an intense and debilitating craving.

By the time I started writing *The Wounded Woman* I was a veteran drinker. I needed alcohol in my body every day to avoid the pain of withdrawal. I was blood for the vampire of addiction.

CHAPTER 46

On the Doorstep of AA

My teaching job at University of Colorado, Denver was exciting. The students were mature since the classes were at night. After class we went out drinking with the art teachers. Then the group that lived in Boulder took the late night bus home.

I also went hiking and cross-country skiing with them. Two especially, Janine and Lara, became my close friends.

Phyllis Kenevan, the muse that introduced me to existentialism, also became my best friend. She was now interested in both Jung and Heidegger. Her husband, Charlie, taught with me in Denver.

At their house I drank more and more. Charlie was in AA and saw my progression into the abyss. One time he asked me to go with him to a Denver jail where an older, nutty student, Ramona, got mad at a store clerk and hit him over the head with her pocketbook. We were able to bail her out of the "clink." Charlie was my first experience of someone in AA.

At this time, I started taking clients. One, a very tall man, told me he had been diagnosed as psychotic, but he wanted to delve into his dreams. I was inexperienced and not alert to danger. I worked well with him. One morning I received a harassing call from a man who made sexual comments. I was scared and wondered who made the call. I didn't think it was my client, but told Charlie because we shared adjoining offices. Gathering up my courage, I went to work and Charlie was there hours earlier than usual. The client came in and didn't sit down. He was tall and towered above me. He told me he was afraid he might murder me; it had happened in one of his dreams. I asked him to tell me his dream. I interpreted it in such a way that showed him he would not kill me. He was relieved and sat down and we continued his session. I was relieved, too, that my innovative idea saved me from harm. I knew Charlie had come in early to help me, if needed. I was grateful for his care and had experienced another AA tenet—to help people whenever possible.

CHAPTER 47

Travels with Shirley

In 1977 I was granted a leave of absence and moved to San Francisco. There I proceeded to get my therapy license and met two important colleagues.

One was Shirley, an adventurous soul. We planned a trip to Peru to go to Machu Picchu. Our plane to Cusco, the gateway to the magnificent sanctuary, was late and we were stranded. No way to Machu Picchu was available, so we decided to head to Bolivia. But the last bus was gone for the day. Just then a small truck arrived; the locals said we could sit in the open back and ride with them. Immune to thoughts of danger, we got in the truck and soon we came to a small village where they left us. We were very tired and found a place to sleep.

The next day Shirley was very sick; I rushed to find a doctor. I didn't speak Spanish but came to understand the truck drivers hadn't stopped at the border. We were in Bolivia illegally! Now I had to explain to authorities why this had happened. I knew we would be in trouble. Somehow I was able to tell them; maybe I looked young and innocent. They stamped our passports and told me where to find a doctor. He diagnosed Shirley with altitude sickness; she just had to rest.

Soon we were able to find a bus to La Paz, 12,264 feet in altitude and the capital of Bolivia. From there we found a way to a boat in Lake Titicaca, said to be the birthplace of the Incas, "The Cradle of the World," and from which emerged the creator of life and the birth of the Sun God.

The voyage across the lake would take us to land so we could take a bus to Cusco and then the sacred valley of Machu Picchu, the spiritual site of the Incas. The Inca people believed the valley reflected the heavenly Milky Way. The valley also contained rich soil that fostered agriculture. The poet and Nobel Prize winner, Pablo Neruda, wrote his famous poem, "The Heights of Machu Picchu," inspired by its magnificence and sacred history.

Next Shirley and I went to the Amazon in Peru. We boarded a slow river boat. Later, Shirley suddenly jumped out of the boat; she was oblivious of the dangerous piranha that lived in the waters. The Amazon River has been named one of the "Seven Wonders of the World," and we received the wonder of one of its scarier lessons.

Finally we ended our trip by going to the Galápagos Islands, home to the giant tortoises and other wildlife wonders. Shirley was an avid animal lover which led us there. The Galápagos was essential to Darwin in his study of evolution. In 1835, he arrived at the Islands and began his observations that would be crucial to developing his theory of evolution by natural selection. Shirley and I wanted to see the numerous species of reptiles, plants, and birds there, including the famous finches that bear his name. As fellow adventurers, we were thankful to see the Galápagos as the site and beginning of our understanding of the evolutionary processes that shape life on our planet.

Shirley and I were adventurers and risk takers, which reflected the adventures I would later make with Keith. Our travels together occurred before I met Keith. Later Keith, Shirley, Shirley's husband, and I met up for dinner. We enjoyed Shirley's sharp and witty sense of humor and she was very down to earth. I tear up now because Shirley died early due to cancer. How sad that I lost such an amazing soul sister so early in life due to a dreaded disease. If Shirley could talk now, she would probably have a witty saying to make me laugh, lighten my load of grief.

CHAPTER 48

Harold and the Misfit Christmas

Harold was another of my adventurous friends. He was a therapist and we had offices in the same building. We became drinking buddies and also went on hikes together.

Harold was gay and liked dressing up as a woman movie star. He took me to a transsexual bar in the Tenderloin where the angry men threw us out since women weren't allowed.

He also introduced me to poppers. Poppers were a drug popular in the gay male community in the 1970s, historically packaged in fragile glass ampoules that were crushed or "popped" for inhalation, used to enhance sexual pleasure or create a euphoric state. Once he tried to chase my stalker away. And another time, Harold and I spent a very lonely and rainy Christmas together. We walked the streets looking for dinner. Nary a restaurant was open. Wet from our hike, we did find a Denny's open. We were forlorn and were misfits who also had to present ourselves as respectable in our professional lives. When it became clear to Harold that I was an alcoholic headed for disaster, he confronted me with this fact. I wrote a new book chapter that the editors wanted at his house. Harold quit drinking when I tried to stop. He said alcohol led to smoking—his deadly addiction.

When AIDS came to the forefront many of his patients died. He couldn't bear all the agony and moved to Thailand and found a lover there.

Later he invited Keith and me to this most beautiful country and took us to temples there. He also arranged for us to stay at the Rose Hotel—actually a famed place for prostitutes in Bangkok. And he took us to a club where the waiters were gay, but who flirted with women. Keith protected himself by sitting behind me while Harold enjoyed his teasing escapade.

Harold arranged for a guide from Laos to take us through the jungle to visit tribal people; the guide was a tall handsome man who played a stunt double for dangerous scenes in movies. But was it really safe to go with him since we had heard of murders happening to tourists on these expeditions? Keith greeted the guide, went into a store with him, and asked which knives he liked best. He pointed to the most lethal knife and Keith bought it for him. In this way Keith gained mutual trust for the guide and ourselves and showed that he was not afraid. We visited the Karen, people who revere elephants, and slept on a raised platform where a baby elephant put his trunk on the platform. Later we rode the elephants and while crossing a river the guide caught a fish with his bare hands. The guide became like a son to us and I wished we could take him home.

CHAPTER 49

Kali Leads Me to AA

Keith: I was thinking of your stalker, Kali, today. I remember your fear. And so you were left to live in dread. Bitter memories.

Linda: Indeed. The incidents of Kali following me reminded me of my father and my childhood fears that he would follow me to school. I was suffering from a PTSD trauma—a repeat of dreaded harassment; an anxiety of which I would never be free. As a child I had a recurring dream: a tall thin man in black was following me over some abandoned railway tracks to catch me before I got home. This same tall thin man in black had appeared in my hashish delusion in Zurich.

The threat of Kali's following me increased my anxiety; I began to drink again to relieve my fears.

On the Saturday morning that I was to give a workshop at the San Francisco Jungian Institute, I saw the dreaded Kali about a block away down the street. I hastily took a Valium hoping to be calm enough to lecture. In the morning session I wasn't doing well. At lunchtime I went upstairs. Wine was on the tables. It was for analysts attending a meeting. I grabbed a glass and gulped it down. Then I reached for another. By now I was in no shape to lecture. Instead, I was about to collapse. A kind colleague phoned my analyst, Don Sandner, and drove me to his office. Don was there waiting for me and stayed with me until I was sober enough to go home. I can't remember how I did get home but knew I was safe inside.

The institute gave me an ultimatum. I needed counsel with an AA sponsor. I had to stop drinking. I knew this and had tried to stop many times. But after about six months of sobriety an event would occur that shook me up and I would reach for a drink. This had happened so frequently that I knew I was just like my father after all. My previous analyst, Joe Wheelwright, had been among the first to confront me. He said: "I'm afraid, my dear, that you are an alcoholic; you simply have to stop drinking." He told me that he had had a drinking problem when young, but it stopped when he was older. Joe Wheelwright was a man with a huge generous heart. I could hear the truth from him. His wife, Jane, also an analyst, had accompanied me to a court hearing in which I was on trial for a DUI. I was given a sentence. Jail for six months or six months of community service. I chose the latter and worked at Muir Woods cleaning urinals, trimming branches, and other such menial work.

I went to AA and knew it worked for many. The people there were all equals. Alcoholism had no regard for class, education, or money. At a meeting there was a circle of love, people sharing their stories, and a series of twelve steps to work to keep sober. The first step is surrender to the fact that I, Linda, am an alcoholic.

Jung once had a patient with a drinking problem so severe that he could not help this man. In all humility Jung told the man, Roland H., that he could not cure this baffling disease. But Jung had a hope that if Roland H. could find others like himself, they could come together, share their stories, finding compassion and spirituality, and this way find recovery. Jung's words reached Bill W., another hopeless alcoholic. Bill W. took those words to heart; he had a vision that the way to be free of this dreaded malady was to find spirituality in a circle of love. And so AA began. Years later Bill W. wrote to Jung thanking him for his humility and wisdom. Jung wrote back saying that the problem lay in mistaking "spirits" for spirit.

CHAPTER 50

Four Relapses Four Miracles

I had so many times when I was able to stop drinking, but within a few months a disturbing incident would occur. And though I tried to fight the deadly urge, I ended by taking a drink. By now it was clear: if I took one drink, I was unable to stop. Four such relapses sent me to hospitals.

Relapse 1: I Am an Alcoholic; Recognized by Another

The first occurred during a ski vacation in Sun Valley. A friend said that Keith and I could stay at her condo. When we arrived we found a wine cellar containing carefully selected bottles of premium wine. We could not resist such a splendid surprise.

We were on vacation after all—what AA would call a "geographic." If I couldn't drink at home while working, surely I could drink somewhere else on a trip. We started drinking and neither of us stopped. By now a few ski days were over. I did try to ski one day, but took a drink to manage vertigo on the chairlift. Back at the condo we ordered more wine. We tried to replace the quality wine with more that matched the careful selection. But once more we drank everything we had ordered.

Finally Keith left to go home. When the maid came to clean, she found me drunk and the place a mess. She called my friend's husband who said to me firmly, "I've ordered an ambulance to take you to the hospital to recover from your relapse." A few days later, when I was released to go home, a doctor came to talk to me. He was an anesthesiologist who had been present when I was admitted. He was kind but firm telling me that he was a recovering alcoholic and in AA. He said that he had no doubt that I, too, was an alcoholic and that AA could help me. He emphasized the severity of my condition.

Relapse 2: My Three Options; I Find Solace in AA

Relapse number 2 occurred a few months later. A new client had described the wonderful day she had sitting at an outdoor table in the sun, eating a gourmet meal, and drinking fine wine. As I heard her, I noticed I was envious. I wanted to enjoy the pleasures she described. My work week was now over and I ordered wine. Although I started with one glass, I kept ordering more. From inside my apartment, I called for delivery each time increasing my orders.

Soon several days passed; my screen door was locked. Keith couldn't get in, but saw the problem. Maybe he felt helpless. He called several of my friends who came trying to convince me to open the screen and go with them to a hospital. I remember Karen Signell crying in desperation. Finally my doctor friend, Bob Clark, was able to persuade me to let him inside. He took me to San Francisco General Hospital to detox. There I encountered nurses and counselors who had read *The*

Wounded Woman. One told me that I knew what I had to do; it was time to actualize what I had written. The psychiatrist in charge spoke to me and said I had only three options. The first was to stop drinking. If I failed to do that, the second was to go mad. And the third was to die. He was mean, without a shred of empathy, definitely a man against whom to rebel.

However I knew I had to stop drinking, but didn't know how.

I called an AA sponsor and went to meetings. Keith and I went to a counselor from the hospital. She was in AlAnon and didn't like Keith; he was angry at me during most of our sessions. Secretly she hoped we would separate. She liked me and had read *The Wounded Woman*. But she was an *Armored Amazon* to whom I didn't relate. I did like AA and found solace there. But my craving for pleasure that once sustained me but now, no more, resumed despite my attempts to embrace recovery.

Keith went with me to what became my "home meeting." My sponsors, Carolyn and Bud, went there, too. Bud told me he thought Keith was also an alcoholic but with a different pattern. He could start drinking and stop on a dime, that was typical for a binge drinker. But I was a maintenance drinker. Once I started I couldn't stop on my own, because the toxins were ingrained in my body.

Relapse 3: Lost in Drink; Recovery Through Love

The third relapse started several months later. I can't remember the cause. Keith and I now lived together deep in the redwoods of Mill Valley. It was said that Joe Dimagio and

Marilyn Monroe had spent their honeymoon there and that The Grateful Dead played music on another occasion. Deer surrounded the house and their goddess, Artemis, was nearby, too. The house was old but was surrounded by windows. A small room with window ledges for crystals made a perfect office. We had a waterbed upstairs and downstairs we got by with a mattress for a couch. We lived in a romantic bohemian style.

One day I took up a drink. As I said I can't remember why or how. A visitor came and found me drunk. She took me to the Adventist Health Hospital in Sonoma. Once again I went through detox. The psychiatric director was very kind. I liked him and believed what he said: "You have three options: you can choose to stop drinking. Or you may go mad. And finally you may die." The same choices that the mean doctor from San Francisco General had given. But these came from a gentle, spiritual man.

Part of the recovery program at Adventist Health was to go to an AA meeting. The room was filled with love. A lawyer was a speaker who told his story. This time I actually felt the love. A miracle happened. A relapse yes, but a way of recovery through love that I still can feel in my heart today.

Relapse 4 : Resentment; a Moral Inventory, and a Lifelong Friend

Why, then, did I have yet another relapse? It happened because I became resentful.

Keith and I were in Aspen to ski. I don't remember why I was angry, but I do remember I took a fateful drink. Keith had given me a beautiful crystal. For some reason I must have wanted something else. In any case I became resentful—the number one cause of addiction. I drank and all know the rest of the story. Once started I couldn't stop. Keith left but called up my mother and also the head of the condo. She called the sheriff and soon I heard a knock at the door. In the meantime I roused myself and called up AA. But the knock came from a health officer named Renick Stevenson. He told me he was a recovering alcoholic and in AA. He planned to take me to a halfway house in Glenwood Springs where many addicts from Aspen were helped. I liked Renick a lot; he was also an artist and a former "beat" in the tradition of Jack Kerouac. He told me he would leave me there for five days until I detoxed. He would visit me once, then bring me back to Aspen at the end of five days.

I didn't like the place and especially not the Gatorade they gave us to drink. But a synchronicity happened there. A man who had been sober for fifteen years had a relapse and came there to recover. While there he went into convulsions and was taken to the nearby hospital. When he returned, he told us his story. With fifteen years sober he thought he was cured. But instead he almost died from convulsions. Alcoholism is described as a progressive disease. Even though a person has not been drinking, the disease progresses in their body, so if one takes a drink it is as though one has been drinking all the time. This man's misfortune was my lesson. I had seen for myself the danger of ever taking a drink again.

Another benefit I received from this place came in the form of a tough woman director. She told me she was an alcoholic and also a cocaine addict, a common occurrence in a town like Aspen. She questioned me thoroughly and asked me about the counseling I had received. I told her that my counselor advised me to work the first three steps of surrender, but said that the fourth step, "the moral inventory," was too soon for me to undertake. The tough woman questioning me said, "That is the problem. You must start on the fourth step now." The fourth step works on resentment which in my case had led to this last relapse. She said, "Your counselor is not an alcoholic. She doesn't know the tricks of this cunning, baffling disease." I knew she was right.

In five days' time, Renick came to pick me up. In Aspen he searched my apartment to make sure I had not hidden booze. I was now free to return home to Keith. And I now had a lifelong AA friend in Renick, a friendship that has endured until this very day.

CHAPTER 51

Crises with Keith

Linda: As I lived with Keith, crises would frequently arrive:

Keith on a Roof Top

I was away in New York and Keith was drinking. He climbed up on the roof of the house. He had phoned his youngest daughter and she phoned me crying. I immediately phoned my AA sponsor, Bud, who said, "Call the fire department and call your analyst. That is all you can do. Let go of worry and enjoy the day." I did as he asked. When the fire department men saw Keith on the roof they recognized him because he worked in ER. They said, "Dr. Chapman, what are you doing on the roof of your house and what is that in your hand?" It was a bottle of vodka. They got him to come down. My analyst also arrived, but he never believed that Keith was drinking. Our analyst did not understand addiction.

Keith Threatens Me

Once in Aspen for the summer, we had a stream of visitors to our studio condo. Now taking an experimental medicine, Keith went crazy. We had an unexpected visitor, the ex-husband of my friend. On a loop hike around Lost Man Lake, Keith took a different route, got ahead of us and, while we were a few thousand feet below on a Boulder field, we saw Keith at the top of the pass. A ferocious lightning storm started and my friend and I hiked back. When we got to the trailhead, we saw that Keith had driven away with our car, leaving us stranded in the dangerous lightning storm. Able to hitch a ride, the friend and I returned to the studio and I decided to leave Keith and go back to Boulder.

I sent a FedEx letter to Keith telling him not to return to Boulder house. He went berserk and phoned my mother, his nephew, and a colleague handling my phone messages. I received worried calls from all three about his threats.

I decided to separate from Keith and stayed separated for six months.

Renick said he would take me to Manitou Springs to run the Pikes Peak Ascent—a thirteen-mile and 7,800-foot climb to 14,107 feet. Such a climb would give me endorphins and help wear off the panic from Keith's threats. Since Keith had planned to run the Ascent, too, I ran extra fast to the top. Renick, who planned to do the entire marathon as well, promised to make sure I would be safe from Keith and drive me back to Boulder. Later I learned that the medicine Keith was taking, combined with his manic phase, probably caused his crazy behavior.

Keith stopped his medicine. And he eventually lured me back with a trip to find wild elephants in the Thailand jungle. We did the trek in Thailand and stayed with the tribe that cared for elephants. Keith now was his usual self.

Keith Gets a Pacemaker

Once again Keith got into trouble while drinking. He got into a fight with a man at the bar. Somehow Keith fell down steps as he went outside. Eventually he was taken to hospital and given a pacemaker. An old girlfriend took him because I was in Aspen trying to write my book on addiction. Sister Anne, a social worker at Napa, called me. We discussed whether I should return home. I decided no, because it would be me acting as codependent. She agreed. Sister Anne was the solid person behind Keith at Napa. I'm sorry I never met her in person.

Keith Quits Drinking

Keith was sometimes very angry with me. His threats sounded serious, but I was not so afraid, I just didn't want to be around his anger. Keith, who was a binge drinker, decided to stop drinking on his own. I think he knew by this time that alcohol would kill him and he credited me for this, even though he did it on his own. Just now I am thinking that maybe he stayed with me, despite times when he was angry that I went away on trips with friends, because ultimately with me he really couldn't drink. He observed, honored my boundary.

CHAPTER 52

The Honeymoon Journey

Linda: Soon after *The Wounded Woman* became a bestseller, Sam Berkholz, the publisher of Shambhala, called me to see if I wanted to write another book. I said that I wanted to write about Rilke, but he said he wasn't interested in it. Then, a few days later, a title sprang to mind. *On the Way to the Wedding* was born in that instant. He liked the title. I had no idea what I would write. I let the creative unconscious have full reign.

I worked with a new editor at Shambhala. Emily Sell was a playful intuitive Muse. She was also a Buddhist devotee of Chögyam Trungpa. Emily and I walked around Boulder where Shambhala was located. We tossed around ideas for the *Wedding* book. We decided to find archetypal characters that were obstacles to authentic growth. We agreed that a commentary on Rilke's quest for the Divine Wedding would be a poetic ending. Jung had written about the wedding of masculine and feminine and its alchemical basis via the union of heaven and earth. The creative time that ensued lay the ground for my next book. *On the Way to the Wedding* became a bestseller and was translated into other languages.

Keith, do you remember how that book became a "Honeymoon Journey" for us? We were going to operas, ballets and films and we had a series of surprises. The artwork we saw inspired chapters for the book by describing archetypal characters that could interfere and prevent a genuine meeting and development of soulmates. We lived with those figures due to our passionate search for knowledge and growth.

One such archetypal character, the Demon Lover, was in *Berlin Alexanderplatz*, directed by Werner Rainer Fassbinder. The film was a fourteen-part television miniseries set in 1920s Berlin and adapted from Alfred Döblin's novel of the same title. Döblin was a Jewish physician who healed the poor in Berlin. He escaped from Germany when Hitler came to power. Döblin saw Hitler as a real life example of the Demon Lover due to his ability to mesmerize people.

Berlin Alexanderplatz was shown at the Castro, a historic San Francisco theater with painted ceilings and an organ, over four days. I remember the color pink stood out, though the film portrayed characters from the underworld—convicts, prostitutes and pimps. They were dark romantic figures. The protagonist, Franz Biberkopf, a common laborer and part-time pimp, has just been let out from prison. He had killed his girlfriend during a crime of passion. Now he wants to change his life. Reinhold, a gangster he meets, sets him up for failure and murders Franz's new love, the gentle Mieze. Franz goes mad. The archetypal figure, Reinhold, was the Demon Lover, who seduces people through addiction and other afflictions and leads them to the ravages of Hell.

We also saw the Demon Lover in the figure of Dracula, the vampire. And we saw all the film versions of Dracula and read Bram Stoker's novel.

We saw Wagner's opera, *The Flying Dutchman*, which portrayed another archetypal character, the Ghostly Lover. This archetype is about an idealized imaginary lover who promises an experience of infinity, a magical union which does not exist in the earthly world. The Ghostly Lover seduces us to live in the realm of possibility without the work of integrating into ordinary daily life. Wagner's Dutchman is a ship captain who dared the devil that he could sail around the Cape of Good Hope, the edge of the world. The devil condemns him to sail ceaselessly without rest; once every seven years he can be on land to try to find a woman who loves him to save him from his lifelong journey. A woman on land hears the legend of the Flying Dutchman and she falls in love. But this love can never be actualized on earth, so she jumps from a cliff into the sea to be with the Dutchman—a love that can only be found in death. Through her sacrifice she redeems the Dutchman and their transfigured forms rise in unison toward the heavens. In this way the libretto ends with "*The Liebestod,*" i.e., the love-in-death motif which promises redemption.

Keith, you and I loved that realm of possibility; we were romantics constantly seeking magical union with people, places and events. We came to understand that relationship requires hard work and patient diligence to make the earth our home.

During this time we went to the ballet, *Swan Lake*, the story of a Prince who falls in love with a beautiful white swan when he sees her change into a lovely woman; she has been bewitched by an evil sorcerer and is condemned to be a swan unless she is saved by a man who pledges eternal love. The prince pledges love, but is tricked when he sees a black swan with whom he also falls in love. Thus he betrays the white swan until he realizes his error. In the end the two briefly unite, but are condemned to *a love in death*. Here Bewitchment is an obstacle to the divine wedding they seek. The tale also points to the figure of Prince Charming who offers material wealth and security—the mate that the Special Princess longs to meet.

When Wagner's four part opera, *The Ring*, came to town, we wanted to see it, but it was sold out. We went to the opera house anyway on the chance we could find a way in. We were graced that evening because a man approached us hoping to sell his tickets. And so began our passion for *The Ring*.

The struggle between love and power is the main theme of the *The Ring*, the fifteen-hour opera. It's an opera about a magical ring, and its home is in the depths of the Rhine river and where it belongs to Nature. There the Rhinegold, a hoard of gold, is revered and guarded by the playful Rhine Maidens. But a dwarf sees the gold and through trickery steals the precious gold ring from them. He uses it to gain wealth and power. Through a series of events the ring is stolen and passes from one creature to another, all of whom want to possess its power. The Ring grants the power to rule the world. Up in the heavens the gods want it, too. Wotan, ruler of gods and men, wants gold to build his empire, Valhalla; he tricks the dwarf into giving up the ring, who in revenge puts a spell upon it that affects any who possess it. Siegfried, Wotan's grandson, is able to slay a dragon that has come into possession of the ring.

Meanwhile Wotan's daughter, the Valkyrie Brunnhilde, has disobeyed him by helping two lovers escape his punishment. Wotan penalizes Brunnhilde by rendering her unconscious and placing her in a ring of fire. Only a man courageous enough to brave the fire and awaken her will be able to save her and be her beloved. Siegfried is that man. He gives Brunnhilde the Ring. Knowing that it belongs to Nature and neither to gods nor men, Brunnhilde returns the Ring to the Rhine Maidens who protect the Ring in Nature assuring the victory of love over power. In so doing she sacrifices her life on Siegfried's funeral fire and the gods and Valhalla are destroyed. A heroine, she surrenders power for love.

Well, Keith, we fell in love with *The Ring.* And we have seen it many times. You have been my Siegfried. You rescued me, your Brunnhilde, from the circle of fire that surrounded me due to my father wound.

PART 4

The Face of Love

"For beauty is nothing but the
Beginning of terror
Which we are barely able to
Endure, and it amazes us so,
Because it serenely distains to
Destroy us.
Every Angel is terrible."

—Rainer Maria Rilke

CHAPTER 53

The Face of God

Linda: I had this dream when in Hawaii at the big island and I wanted to get up at dawn to see the sunrise over the volcano in 1979.

I wake at dawn and go to the window to see the sunrise over the volcano. Instead I am looking at the face of God who is a huge icy glacier of vibrant colors—purple, electric blue, red. It is terrifying and so powerful it knocks me back across the room to the floor. I'm amazed I'*m still alive.*

When I wake up I'm on the floor where "God" threw me and I remember I was told never to look God directly in the face.

This is one of the most powerful dreams I have ever had.

CHAPTER 54

Our Secret Knowledge

Jean: My goodness, Linda, your dream of seeing the Face of God is amazing. Thrilling actually.

I think that's a rare dream of you coming into your true self, the being you were meant to be. Ha, excuse me if I'm talking to you, a Jungian analyst, outside of my place. Old Jean Le Fou just likes to talk.

You told me of your relapses, so painful. And I'm struck by something, a commonality that seems to occur for you. As each crisis occurs, alcohol subdues you, takes you away, the horrible falls of addiction, each time the angels hear your call. They rush to you to find and help you. Do you see that? As you crash, are helpless, others, Keith, Don Sandner, Carolyn and Bud, Karen Signell crying in desperation, Gloria Gregg, Bob Clark, Charlie, Harold… They come to find you, offer help, sometimes so that you are just not alone. Because they may feel a bit helpless, too. But they come to you, in your anguish, to form a sacred circle. Like a secret prayer around you.

I'm especially in wonder at Officer Renick Stevenson's helping you in Glenwood Springs. This seems to come from a wonderful place in him. He doesn't know you, but knows your plight. He has suffered the same way as you, alcoholic relapse, and he hears of you and responds. Not in a formal way, not distanced for safety. He comes and takes you in his car to the safety he knows you need. A responding person, not formal or rigid, bends to lift you, give his hand, take you to safety and healing. I think Renick Stevenson is a marvel, a wonderful being in this world. Oh, I just want to celebrate what he did for you. Something you could feel, could heal with, could recover under.

I snooped on the internet to find out a little more about Renick. And he was an alcoholic, a painter, a poet in the Beat generation. He is a human with talents, secret aspirations, a striving life, who saved himself, was part of AA, and here, when you needed him, he shows up as a correctional officer knowing how to help you, reaches out to you. Walks you to safety.

I find that marvelous, amazing, even a touch of a miracle.

Just as I found your book and it saved me, and forty years later, I wrote you a letter of thanks, and it found you…and the miracle is we became friends. And, as things go, you and I have these wonderful meetings and conversations together. As you share your life, and I mine. All because I had to write you my thanks.

So Linda, here, I'll stop talking your ear off.

Linda: What beautiful, beautiful words. Spoken with passion. Thank you for such a wonderful talk. I am very grateful for our friendship.

Jean: *Bien sûr. Nous sommes des parfaits amis,* Linda! I'm grateful as well.

So Linda, I draw this tarot card for you:

Daath!

Oh Linda, this is the secret card of the Tarot. It is only in this deck. No other deck has it. And I've only drawn this card once before. It is a mysterious card, generally unknown to others, a curious part of the Kabbalah, the Tree of Life.

Daath is the point of unification within the Tree of Life, where all ten sephiroth (aspects of the divine) converge. It represents knowledge, perception, skill; discernment, understanding, wisdom. Things we secretly have within us.

In this case today, Linda, it tells us of our hidden knowledge that we as humans have a super power. We live with an ability that is universal in us, a power that can change everything in a life. That power that Daath tells us of today!

And that power is that we humans, as animals, care for others, for *all* around us. We care for our families, our friends, people we don't even know, we care for flowers, butterflies, animals in need, small as voles and mice large as giraffes and whales. Our caring knows no limits. It is secretly what we humans are, and here I give you this secret knowledge from Daath. We are animals that care for all…*across the stars!*

So Linda, if you will oblige me, just as I contacted you so long ago to thank you for my saved life, I ask you now: Will you now contact Renick Stevenson, who so long ago reached out to you with his care, tell him he did well?

This is your Daath assignment. Write to him, and I will send the letter to him. We both will reach out from Daath.

Linda's letter to Renick, sent to Jean:

Dear Renick,

It's Linda, I haven't talked with you in so long. I think it was at my seventy-fifth birthday lecture. I think of you often and your caring help during that difficult time.

I say it plainly, Renick, thank you for saving me. You understood my problem, you saw me, and you cared. You took me to a safe place, the halfway house, so I could recover. I was lucky to meet you. And here you turned out to be a wonderful painter and poet. What fantastic synchronicity to have met you when I was in need. I would love to talk with you and add your picture to a book I'm writing.

I moved to San Francisco two years ago. And now I'm writing a book, and, of course, you are in it! You are in it as one who loves and cares for others. And I thank you, Renick, for your gifts to me. I hope you are happy and painting.

❤ Love,
Linda Schierse Leonard—just Linda to you, dear Renick!

CHAPTER 55

Creativity and the Veil of Addiction

SERENITY PRAYER
God, grant me the serenity to accept the things I cannot change,
Courage to change the things I can,
And wisdom to know the difference.

Now is the time to write about addiction and creativity. But what should I call it? A dream gave me the answer.

An arsonist, an angry red-haired rebellious man, threatened to burn down my retreat, a log cabin nestled in the dark quiet of the woods. I was angry too. Resentfully I told this man to "burn down the house." Flippantly he tossed a match into the house, setting the place ablaze. I realized that I would be held responsible for the fire, for I held in my hands an implicating book. Then out of the house came a kindly man, who showed me a book cover—with the word WITNESS printed boldly on it. It was he who saved the house from burning down.

From the dream came the title for my book:

Witness to the Fire: Creativity and the Veil of Addiction.

As I wrote, I realized the "witness" image referred to the survivors—the recovering people who shared their stories. Each bears witness to the flight, fall, and recovery from the hellfire of addiction and also to the fire of the creative process, the struggle to endure the purging fire of spiritual recovery, and to the work to re-create a new being.

The Flight is the initial stage of the addictive process, which is seductive. In this phase we fly high, just as we do in the early soaring of creative inspiration.

The Fall is the descent into darkness. This is the ominous stage of possession in which the inner patterns solidify, turn cold, hard, and threatening. In the creative process this is when we feel blocked, criticized and tempted to abandon our work. But this darkness must be faced in order to transform the destructive course and to create.

The Creation is the turning point where wounds are accepted, understood and transformed: this is where healing can occur and life can be created anew.

I turned to the etymology of addiction. The Latin word for addict, *addictus*, means to devote, surrender, deliver over, or give oneself up habitually. Although it was used often in a pejorative sense, originally it had a spiritual meaning—*dedication to the gods*—stemming etymologically from "*addicere,*" to say. Thus inherent in the meaning of addiction is the sense of bearing witness to creative energies. In the human condition there exists two archetypal figures—the Demon Lover and the Creative Daimon. The challenge is to devote ourselves to choose the call to create, i.e. the Creative Daimon. Many artists see this struggle—the call to live in the tension between good and evil and that art reveals this universal struggle. The Russian film director, Andrey Tarkovsky, said, "The aim of art is to prepare a person for death, to plough and harrow his soul, rendering it capable of turning to good."

Generosity is a way we can distinguish between the Demon Lover and the Creative Daimon. The Demon Lover sucks our blood until we become one of the "living dead" as in the story of Dracula, the vampire. In contrast creativity is regenerative and gives to us and to the world transformation towards wholeness. A miracle happens through creativity: receiving becomes giving and giving becomes receptivity.

The Russian poet, Alexander Pushkin, writes:

Like a corpse I lay in the waste land
And I heard God's voice cry out:
Arise prophet, and see and hear,
Be charged with my will—
And go out over seas and lands
To fire men's hearts with the word.

As I wrote I discovered archetypal characters in myself that operate in both addiction and creativity. Here I describe them briefly to remember them for myself and others. They are detailed in *Witness to the Fire* for greater understanding. If you struggle with addiction, you must look for these.

The Hostage is in denial and becomes victim to the prison of addiction. In creativity we become "hostage" to opening and becoming whole by living in the tension of opposites that comprise human existence.

The Moneylender offers to lend us a high, a fast rush to ecstasy. But we are charged with a large debt to be paid later. Inspiration is the "loan" we experience in creativity with the understanding that we can give back the gift through the struggle of artistic work.

The Gambler takes the risk for excitement and to gain something for nothing, but eventually returns empty-handed and in debt. In creativity we take the risk of light, love, and hope for transformation and serenity.

The Romantic longs for ecstasy that is eternal, but encounters the limits of our finite existence. In creativity the Romantic's longing is akin to the mystic's search to be aflame with love for the divinity within us.

The Underground Man wants eternal love, but turns cynical and resentful that life requires attention to limits. In creative life the Underground Man dares to descend into the "Dark Night of the Soul" and endures the fire of divinity.

The Outlaw is at odds with society. By breaking the laws of conventionality he may end up in prison. In creative life, however, the Outlaw learns that rebellion can overcome strict tyrannical rule and to fight for justice.

The Trickster in addiction can lead to relapses. In creative life the Trickster often steals our ego stance leaving us naked but open to change.

The Madwoman has anger that can turn into paranoia which can kill and lead to imprisonment in a locked ward. But the

Madwoman who descends into darkness can transform her rage into the creative fire of transformation.

The Judge who often is driven by a thirst for perfection can criticize a person severely and render them helpless before his court. But in creativity we need to make judgments that distinguish between the good and the bad.

The Killer can murder love and the inner child. However, in the creative act we need the Killer to "kill off" old habits and obstacles that prevent new ways of life and artistic endeavor.

The World's Night describes the addictive descent into a lust for greed and possession that leads to world war and holocaust. Facing and eradicating the evil within and outside in society is needed to pave a path for peace.

Witness to the Fire was published in 1989 and also met with success, although to a lesser degree than my two prior books. It was translated into Italian and was used widely in hospitals that dealt with addiction. For me it was a catharsis.

My greatest thrill was the recommendation from Athol Fugard, the anti-apartheid South African playwright, novelist, and film director who himself had to give up drinking. About *Witness to the Fire,* he wrote, "The most perceptive and compassionate study I have yet read of the problem of addiction. Essential reading for anyone who has dealt with or is dealing with addiction."

Painting of the Black Madonna.
Black Madonna, Publishing License and Copyright 2026
Shutterstock-2368616523

CHAPTER 56

Our Pilgrimage to The Black Madonna

Linda: Keith, we have made so many spiritual pilgrimages together. One of the most profound has been to honor The Black Madonna.

The Black Madonna was associated with miracles, saving nations from invasions, representing the Virgin Mary's power of wisdom and protection.

I first encountered her in an area where I hiked in Einsiedeln, Switzerland, at the Benedictine Abbey. Her image appeared in cathedrals across Europe. You and I visited her in Monserrat outside of Barcelona. And I visited her again in France in the Camarque and Rocamandour and also Cuba. The virgin of Guadalupe was another of her manifestations.

But the greatest of our pilgrimages to honor her was in Czestohova, Poland.

The Black Madonna held the sorrows of existence through her strength of survival. In Poland her image was held high during an invasion by the Swedes and bore a scar on her cheek like a tear from the battle. The Poles believe she enabled them to survive. Her dark face linked her to pre-Christian times and to early goddesses in Egypt. She was also often carved from wood that accounted for her dark appearance.

She held within herself the power of both dark and light, transcending division of the opposites. It was said that when priests tried to remove her physically from the church, she would return miraculously to her original home. For you and I, her greatest strength was contained in her sorrow of compassion that healed the wounds of humankind.

The day we went to Czestahova to find her turned out to be a special feast day. On the way back in the train a man sat with us in our compartment. He was a doctor specializing in treating cancer. You told him that you had a melanoma but had countered it with running. He said that research had shown that aerobic breathing helped heal the cancer. We felt blessed and that his presence was a synchronicity related to our pilgrimage to the Black Madonna. She was indeed a miraculous feminine presence—another *Face of Love.*

CHAPTER 57

Symphony of Sorrowful Songs

One day a disc jockey decided to broadcast a new classical work by an unknown Polish composer. The music struck a sacred chord to listeners—so powerful that drivers stopped their cars to hear it. They were captivated by Górecki's *Symphony of Sorrowful Songs*. The symphony suddenly rose to the top of the popular music charts and stayed there for months, surprising the composer and other musicians around the world. Sacred minimalist music, previously unknown, broke through a ceiling to become the most popular classical symphony ever recorded.

Górecki's Symphony No. 3 became a phenomenon for which music lovers had been craving. The symphony's CD release, recorded by the London Sinfonietta, sold over a million copies in Britain and the U.S. The unknown and meagerly paid Polish composer received a first royalty check of over $100,000, so large and surprising, Górecki kept it in his wallet afraid to cash it.

How the unknown Górecki symphony became recorded by two Americans is nothing short of a miracle.

In 1991 the contemporary composer, Ned Rorem, suggested to David Zinman, head conductor of the Aspen Music Festival, that Górecki's symphony, composed fifteen years earlier, would become important. As the story goes, at first Zinman was skeptical but decided to take a risk. The singer would be Dawn Upshaw, the renowned American soprano of classical song. Zinman did the recording in a subway in London to try to make the sound as though it was in a cathedral. He didn't expect it to be spectacular.

But miracles do exist and *Symphony of Sorrowful Songs* touched the hearts of listeners. Górecki himself was surprised and said the music must have brought something missing and needed to people.

The symphony was written to commemorate the memory of those lost during the Holocaust. Its major themes are motherhood and separation through war. Its three movements are slow, contemplative, and haunting. The first and third depict a mother who has lost a child while the second depicts a child separated from a parent.

The libretto for the first movement comes from a fifteenth century lament. The second movement comes from the words of a teenage girl written on the wall of a gestapo prison cell in Zakopani, at the foot of the Tatra mountains, to call for the protection of the Virgin Mary. The text of a Silesian folk song describing the pain of a mother searching for a son killed in the Silesian Uprisings comprises the third movement.

Keith, hearing the *Symphony of Sorrowful Songs* touched us deeply and gave us hope to continue our search for the divine during hard parts of life, our journey through the Dark Night of the Soul.

Keith: Linda, when I heard the final movement of the symphony, I understood why people stopped. It is the very voice of sorrow itself. I could not drive through tears.

Keith and Linda happy together.

CHAPTER 58

Who You Are to Me

Linda: Dear Keith, in my initial dream for Jungian analysis one of the men hanging from the rafters shouted "Get me down! Get me down." I realized he was like Zorba the Greek, and he was also like my paternal grandfather. The dream showed how important Zorba was to my life; he was also a repressed part of my Self.

Zorba was a Dionysian character: he loved to dance and he loved women. Moreover, you, Keith, were a Zorba-like man. To be with you, I had to love your Zorba, too.

The Greek author, Nikos Kazantzakkis, wrote a book about Zorba—a novel about a man of sixty who decides to mentor a younger man who has been cut off from his Dionysian side. Might this younger man be a reflection of the "Young Man With a Lack" in my dream? In the 1964 film adapted from the novel, Zorba encourages the younger man to dance with him on a beach. They dance side by side with their arms touching each other's shoulders. Zorba almost loses his footing but recovers his balance preventing a fall. They laugh together in unison; the two are able to dance as one.

Keith, I know you treated Anthony Quinn who portrayed Zorba during its filming. And I presented this playful scene of Zorba dancing at the end of my memorial service for you.

If I love an author, I try to make a pilgrimage to his or her grave. And so I went to Crete to pay homage to Kazantzakis at his burial site. I was rewarded when I learned that it was possible to hike down a steep ravine from the White Mountains ten miles to the Libyan Sea. If time permitted a swim in the sea was possible. From there one could catch a boat to another shore and take a bus back to the site of the trailhead. I spent seven hours descending the Samaria Gorge and breathing in the perfume of the Cyprus, the maples, oaks, and pine forests, the white peony, plum purple flowers and other plants. I wondered how often Kazantzakis had traversed this sacred site.

Keith, you are my Zorba!

CHAPTER 59

David Bohm's Peaceful Dialogue

Linda: Keith, you loved the work of the physicist, David Bohm, and you carried his book wherever you went in Aspen. Then you actually had a chance to meet and thank him in person in Prague. I introduced you to him.

Two years earlier I was invited to be part of a weeklong Think Tank that focused on the topic of addiction while using a group process of "Peaceful Dialogue"—a free flowing way of relating to others that Bohm hoped could help people reach a common understanding, and experience each other's point of view non-judgmentally. His hope was to solve crises in communication with which society is faced by attending to thought as a process and to be able to listen in order to respond to new creative perceptions. He hoped to go beyond self-defensive prejudice which blocks the ability to listen freely. This requires that no decisions be made, to suspend judgments, to be as honest and transparent as possible, and to build on each other's ideas, thus creating something new together. A goal is for the group to have a better understanding of itself.

The group was composed of four writers on addiction of whom I was one, some Buddhist scholars, and others involved with group process. While there was a high degree of judgment around the addiction topic, I had the opportunity to speak with Bohm; he was very interested in my understanding of Heidegger. I found him to be a beautiful, gentle soul, and will never forget the open way he spoke with me.

So, Keith, I was very happy to be able to help you meet such a whole and peaceful person.

CHAPTER 60

Krzysztof Kieslowski Reveals Soul

Keith: Linda, while we are here in Melbourne for your lecture, I see there's a retrospective of Kieslowski films on now. Isn't that the director you were so ecstatic about back in New York? Let's spend the rest of our time here seeing as many Kieslowski films as we can. I'd love to see these films with you. We may never be able to see them where we live in the U.S.

Linda: Yes, you remembered! And what a synchronicity! Of all the film directors in the world, Krzysztof Kieslowski touched my soul in the deepest way.

I encountered his films by chance. I was in New York and had one day left before I needed to return home when I happened to notice a program at the Museum of Modern Art devoted to the films of a new unknown Polish director, Kieslowski. They were part of his television miniseries called *The Dekalog* inspired by the Ten Commandments. That day *Commandment 4*, *Honor Thy Father and Thy Mother* and *Commandment 5*, *Thou Shalt not Kill* were scheduled.

Each installment was a one-hour film set in a housing project in 1980s Warsaw. They portrayed characters confronted by ethical dilemmas. The script was co-written by Kieslowski and Krzysztof Piesiewicz, a lawyer, who proposed the project to Kieslowski. Kieslowski directed each installment complete with the epic, uplifting music by Zbigniew Preisner. Musical masterpieces! And a different cinematographer was hired to shoot each of the films.

Kieslowski wanted to portray the hardships faced by Polish society while avoiding political issues that would be fodder for censors. He planned not to use the names of the commandments; instead the viewer would be thrown into the paradoxes that each film theme presented.

Released during 1989 and 1990, *The Dekalog* received international praise, including the Best Foreign Series BAFTA award, and the French Cinema Critics announced it as one of the greatest films of all time.

Keith, when I saw *Commandments 4* and *5,* I did not know about their success. The film about "honoring father and mother" had a unique twist and involved an incestual longing of a daughter for her stepfather. I was thrust into the dilemma of each of the characters. The episode on *Thou Shalt Not Kill* involved a young man who murdered a taxi driver, but whose jury faced the controversial death penalty. This film later was responsible for Poland stopping the use of capital punishment! I left *The Dekalog* thinking that this unknown director was truly a genius and I hoped I would be able to see the remaining films another time.

Keith: And here we are! I love to be thrown into a paradox. *The Dekalog* sounds just right for me. And I see they are also showing the premiere of a new film, *The Double Life of Veronique*. I've heard of it. Using two identical characters in a film, as an archetypal figure of "The Double" intrigues me… I see it often in client dreams and in so many artworks that we like.

Linda: Ha, we do match and are inspired by the same art.

———

Indeed, Kieslowski's film, *The Double Life of Veronique* became my favorite of all his films. *The Double Life* is about two young women whose lives are soulful mirrors to one another. Although they have never met, each feels there is a mysterious Other for whom they have been searching. They are born on the same day, at the same time. Both are singers and must choose between their gift of song and a boyfriend. Both are born with dangerous heart conditions.

One, Weronika, is born in Poland while the other, Veronique, is born in France. In celebration, the Polish Weronika's mother holds her baby girl up to the heavens to see the sun and the stars in the sky. With reverence, the French Veronique's mother kneels down showing her baby the earth with all of its fragrances. Tragically, both mothers die when their daughters are three. Their fathers are warm and seek to heal their daughters with love.

The Veronicas grow having a strange sense of their unknown double. One day in Kraków's old town center, the Polish Weronika sees a woman who looks just like her board a

French tourist bus. From this bus, the French Veronique takes a photo of the square unaware that her camera has caught the Polish Weronika at its center. And that is as close to meeting as the two Veronicas will get. The *Doubles* never meet in the earthly world. But each suffers an inexplicable longing for a part of herself that remains unknown.

The Polish Weronika has the gift of song; she remains true to her vocation choosing to become a concert singer, even though this stresses her heart and threatens her life. The French Veronique, learning of the identical dangers of singing to her heart, chooses to sacrifice her singing as a career to safeguard her love relationship with another.

Music unites the two women although neither knows of the other. One day singing a solo at a concert, the Polish Weronika's singing is extraordinary; the music fills the soul of all who hear it, even as she has a heart attack and dies on the spot. And coincidentally, her mystical double, the French Veronique, hears and is tempted to sing the same magnificent music—but knowing from a cardiogram that her heart condition cannot endure it, she chooses to not sing, so that she might seek romance with a talented puppeteer. Later she realizes the puppeteer is taking advantage of her. She then chooses to value her own integrity rather than remain in a longing for a man she cannot trust. She forsakes all and returns home to be with her father—returns home to find her true herself. With Veronique reflecting outside their cottage, the film ends as she pauses to touch a sturdy tree trunk that puts her back in touch with her earthly home and the great Tree of Life. She hears a stunning rise of majestic music, a marvelous sound that overwhelms all who hear. A singing beauty beyond compare. And this otherworldly singing reveals the soul to the listeners and brings to the audience a belief that all are indeed part of a greater whole. Kieslowski's film leaves us knowing that, like Rilke's famous dictum, Song is Existence.

Linda: Keith, we did experience the mystical power of the film and I shed tears for the death of the Polish Weronika with whom I identified.

Keith: I fell in love with both of these pure-hearted girls who also represented feminine parts of myself. I must say, Linda, they reminded me of you, who is constantly searching for transformation and for ways to help your readers and clients to be true to themselves.

Linda: Thank you, if that is true. I want to tell you two stories of viewer reactions that Kieslowski later encountered. Once at a Paris screening, a young woman came to Kieslowski and told him that she did not know there was a Soul; but after seeing *The Double Life of Veronique* she now had experienced Soul. Kieslowski remarked that it was worth all the difficulty of making the film for that young woman to feel the reality of the Soul!

Another time at a screening in Berlin, a mother and daughter approached him. They said that although they shared a room, they had never hugged each other. But now they held each other in their arms! Again Kieslowski rejoiced: "This is why I work so hard to make a film; the joining of souls makes it worthwhile."

Keith: I think I would like this Kieslowski as a person. He is not afraid to descend into the abyss which holds creativity if one dares to tread there. And he is a modest man. As you know I go into the abyss myself when I work with psychotic patients.

Linda: The music is heavenly; every time I hear it I shed tears. And whenever I have a creative block I listen and its transcendence breaks through.

Keith: Yes, I am moved by the music, and a protagonist who cannot escape her destiny, just like you and I cannot escape our vocation to be healers and the commitment our soulmate relationship requires.

I so admire Veronique, this compassionate young woman choosing who she will be, and at what cost. And through Kieslowski's vision, his film helps her and us to transform and find Soul.

Linda: We are lucky; each time we have seen Kieslowski films, they always restore us. Kieslowski has a special place in my heart.

CHAPTER 61

Viva Venezuela

Linda: Keith dear, when we were asked to both lecture in Venezuela, we had no idea how much fun that trip would be. The invitations came from Dr. Luis Sanz, Director of Jungian training, whose group were enamored of my book, *Meeting the Madwoman*. They had even translated it into Spanish themselves. Luis asked you to present how you worked with patients to a group of psychiatrists at the hospital where he was affiliated.

Luis later talked to me about your presentation and how amazed they were about what you did. A "difficult" psychiatrist was present during your talk and the others were worried he would cause a problem. Of course, you didn't know this and went to the blackboard to start. First you wrote your name and listed all your accomplishments, which were many. But then you took an eraser and removed everything you had written until the blackboard was blank. Standing by the empty slate, you said, "This is who I am and where I start from. Everything I erased was ego." All the psychiatrists were surprised. The "difficult" colleague's hand shot up and Luis and the others were concerned. You motioned to him to speak. He said, "At last I can identify with what you have done. I thought I was alone. Thank you, Dr. Chapman."

Luis and the others were relieved and afterwards laughed about their anxiety; they were impressed at your brilliant performance. You, Dear Heart, are like a magician and one never knows what you will pull out of that hat.

My own symposium on the *Madwoman* archetype went well. I delineated Madwoman characters that can act destructively: *The Mad Mother* (including *The Ice Queen, and The Devouring Mother*), *The Caged Bird*, *The Rejected Lover*, *The Bag Lady*, and *The Martyr* —destructive ways of being all stemming from anger at the patriarchy. Then I spoke of creative woman characters like *The Muse*, *The Recluse*, *The Revolutionary*, *The Visionary*... Women who were often called "mad" by paternalistic tyrants. I gave examples from history and everyday life.

Linda laughs: That Venezuelan audience loved talking about the Madwoman.

Keith, I honestly had never intended to write a book on the Madwoman since I put a chapter on her in *Witness to the Fire*. But, when in New York at a cafe, Madwoman patterns interrupted my meal, I quickly wrote them down on a scrap of paper. I also knew my new editor at Bantam had urged me to write about this crazy female character. Moreover, I remembered the Balian shamaness' words: "*Invite her to lunch*." So the book was born, became a success, made the bestseller list, and was even translated into multiple languages.

After our talks, a big surprise was in store for you and me. Luis had arranged a trip down into the jungles near the Amazon to see if we could locate any practicing shamans. Elated, off we travelled with Luis and his wife, Nancy, a world authority on diabetes, and a small group of students, as we headed South. We arrived in the Guiana Shield area, home to the *tepuis*, the table-top mountains and sometimes called "The Lost World." We didn't find any shamans, but we did see a lot of waterfalls and had a lot of fun. We ate together and played together; Luis and his entourage were always laughing. They loved you, Keith, in a way that no other group had.

Luis had supervised under me when he did some of his training in San Francisco. What a provident meeting. He understood me in a way that most colleagues did not. He understood you, too, Keith.

His warmth was infectious and so was Nancy's warmth. I am forever grateful to the forces of destiny that enabled our lives to touch each other.

Keith: *Viva Venezuela!*

Keith and Linda talking about leprechauns in Ireland.

CHAPTER 62

Ireland and the Mystery Man

Ireland, The Last Trip Abroad

—For Keith Chapman from ♣ Linda

Sweetheart
You surprised me in New York
the night before we left for Ireland

The hotel room door opened
and I saw a Mystery Man
one I hadn't seen for awhile
You wore a black raincoat
over a black suit

You were smiling
happy to see my surprise
You might have stepped out
of a Graham Greene novel
You thrilled me like you did
in our early days together

Later, in Ireland, we
stayed at a hotel on the
Dingle peninsula
where I was invited to
speak at a conference

The ravishing beauty
of the countryside
filled our lives—the jagged coast,
lush greenery and ancient sites
enfolded us

We felt the presence
of the fairies there
People were drawn to you
as they often are
Your mother had an
Irish name, Duffy
You felt at home
with your ancestors
from times long ago.

I'm so glad you were
able to partake
of Irish lore on this,
your last trip abroad.

Linda and her analyst Don Sandner.

CHAPTER 63

Death of an Analyst

Linda: *Monsieur Jean Le Fou!* Good to see you, Jean. You've come to visit your favorite neighbor… And widow! This morning, I have an old dream I want to share with you.

The Dream: Don Sandner and I are hiking in the Canyon Lands of Utah. We have to pass through sheer tight canyon walls that are pink-brown in color. We come to a clearing and Don is ahead of me. He crosses a stream to the other side with green grass. I start to cross but Don holds up his hand and says, "Not yet." I know he has crossed into the next world, but is telling me it is not my time yet to cross over.

I had the dream after Don died about twenty-five years ago. I have done conscious active imaginations with it by trying to cross over to Don and also Keith. Usually the current is too strong and I can't quite make it. Don and Keith are holding their hands out to help me. The last few times I'm able to reach Keith's hand and I think I can make it.

I think this must go in the last section of my new book, but am not sure how to title it, and if I should say more about Don. He is the one who led the Bali trip, where Keith first chose me. He is both very imaginative but also very solid and grounded. He is my last analyst and I wish I could work with him now. He finds meditation blissful. I haven't been able to meditate.

Jean: Meditate? On these Faces of Love? *Mais Oui!* Close your eyes, smile, be you. Let's do it now. And here is your card of the day. Just hold it.

The Nine of Water: The Rainbow Mirror

It means go now and meet them. A safe journey.

Linda and Keith hiking together.

CHAPTER 64

At 75 I Chose Keith

The Boulder Friends of Jung invited me to give a big lecture. I said yes and that I would present Terrence Malick's film *The Tree of Life*. They asked me to lecture on another topic since the film might be too difficult for their audience. I said I really wanted to present the film. We went back and forth about the topic, but my mind was made up to discuss the film.

They chose a date, October 12th, not knowing this was my birthday and a big one; I would be seventy-five.

The synchronicity of the lecture date with my turning seventy-five was too big to ignore. So I said, "Okay. I will lecture about me, *at seventy-five*."

I started by playing Górecki's *Symphony of Sorrowful Songs*. Then I showed some pictures of my mother and grandmother—two very strong women in my childhood. I also showed a clip of Kurasawa's film *Dersu Usala* about a Goldi hunter of the Nanai tribe in the wilderness of Kamchatka, who helps a team of Russian cartographers learn how to follow tracks in the dense forest—a metaphor for the way we learn how to follow the markers of our fate.

I traced for the audience the way my life had followed a path that led to the interweaving of my three careers. And I thanked Keith who was present for being my soulmate.

The lecture hall was packed. Renick was there and made a tribute to our friendship! I realized I could start writing my book on aging.

After the lecture, we went to eat. I noticed Keith did not look well. I asked him to come to Aspen to see our doctor there. At the doctor's appointment, she told him he had an enlarged prostate, and insisted that he go to a urologist. This led to his diagnosis of Alzheimer's, about which I was in denial. I tried to care for him myself, but I couldn't control him. The social worker insisted that he needed to be in a nursing home. I felt this was a betrayal, but I had no choice. Luckily I found a good skilled nursing facility, Balfour.

Now I couldn't pursue my writing. I had to get him Medicaid and veteran's benefits which required dealing with bureaucracies and other practical tasks. Keith had no savings of his own.

I also decided to use my own savings, against the advice of the social worker and the Balfour administration. They said I should take care of myself and put him in a Medicaid facility.

Keith did well adjusting to the skilled nursing home and saw himself as the unit's doctor. My money ran out and I put my beloved Aspen condo up for sale. Luckily there was a buyer. And so I was able to keep Keith at Balfour since they didn't accept Medicaid.

I had to sacrifice my plans to write. The practical duties took all my energy. I was desperate. Friends urged me to put Keith in a Medicaid home. But I wanted him to be in a place where he was loved.

And so at seventy-five I chose Keith ahead of my own life.

I do not regret my decision even though it made me anxious and depressed. To this day I know I am grateful that I was able to care for my soulmate, Keith.

On Keith's last day on Earth the staff, students and many others poured into Keith's room and thanked him for the creative call that he had inspired in them. Keith's daughters, Karen and Cathy, and his grandson, Josh, were with him, too. The love in that room for my soulmate, Keith, surrounded him until he took his last breath.

CHAPTER 65

When Song Transcends Separation

Linda: Sweetheart, we shared so many passions. Film was one of the greatest and we loved the relationship of cinema and Psyche up to the very end of our life together. I feel your presence whenever I see a great film today. We are holding hands, sitting in the dark with strangers united by a common bond to experience a work of art that can change their lives and can take them to the depths of their hearts.

Kieslowski's film *Blue* took us on that journey to work through loss, grief, and despair and to heal through answering the call to create.

Julie, the protagonist played by Juliet Binoche, has lost her child and husband in a car accident. She awakens in a hospital and tries to kill herself by swallowing pills. Thwarted in this attempt, she breaks glass in anger. Upon release from the hospital she decides to flee from her life by moving far away from her home. Her husband had been composing a concerto for the unification of Europe. She was helping him compose the music and only she can finish it.

In her despair of defiance, she refuses to complete the concerto by detaching herself from her past. But wherever she is she cannot escape the music. Through a series of synchronous events she is forced to confront the call. In a cafe she hears the music played by a street musician. I felt this was an encounter with Orpheus, who plays the song in his flute. Eventually she accepts the fate that she must complete the concerto. The music is a living character in the film and is overwhelming with emotion that makes her feel alive. As she composes, her life flashes before her and she surrenders to her task, realizing that the power of the music is greater than her loss, and is an embodiment of love.

Blue brought me to tears and reminded me of my own attempts to escape my call to create and wallow in my despair.

We left the film with hope restored by living with Julie's transformation.

And now that we are separated by your death, I can still be with you in song that transcends the separation of the soul in different realms.

Collage of Linda and her Mother.

CHAPTER 66

Mother Death

Linda:
Dear Mom,

I'm so sorry I didn't get back to you in time for your death. I had a plane ticket for the next day to arrive on your birthday. You called me in the morning and said strangers were in your room and your bags were packed for a journey. I knew what that meant. But then you got angry at me and all my old complexes came back.

I was in Aspen with hiking friends so we went on a hike to a lake near Mount Sopris. At the lake we saw a strange sight:

a snake was swallowing a lizard alive. I knew this was a sign of your death so we hurried home. When I called the hospital they said you had just died. My cousin, Sister Catherine, had been with you and told you she wasn't strong enough to care for you at home. She left for a half hour and when she came back you were dead.

I felt terrible that I wasn't there for you in your last day.

But later I had two reassuring dreams that you were okay in the next realm.

In the first dream you owned a restaurant. The colors were pink and you were dressed in a rose pink outfit that was your favorite color. You were in a good mood so I knew you were safe and happy.

The second dream was puzzling. I had to go through a dangerous neighborhood to get to your house. When I got there, it was on a corner and had become a historic museum devoted to you. A statue of you was in front. You were in the form of a very large silver lizard—a very archetypal figure. On your death day I had seen a snake swallow a lizard. I thought of the color of silver in alchemy. Silver means protection. And is associated with the moon. It brings harmony and balance. *Lizard* means survival, adaptability and regeneration. This is you, Mom, and you were honored with the museum attesting to your qualities. I'm still left with this strange meaning.

Mom, I'm so sorry I wasn't there for you. I wish I had taken you on more trips. Asked you more questions.

You were a wonderful Mom for me as a child. Warm and nurturing. You were a heroine in my childhood. But when I became more adult in adolescence you couldn't understand who I was. You got angry at me for not staying with you. It was your anger I couldn't take. So I stayed away unable to be near your anger.

Keith admired your strength and teased you. He knew you were a survivor, someone who knew how to deal with life's problems. He told me he knew how to deal with my depression and proposed a trek in Patagonia. It worked. The effort to do the trek broke my depression. We also went to Easter Island and attended a Catholic mass where the statues were the Island's angels and the priest had a great basket of fruit. The service was joyful.

Mom, I'm sorry I couldn't deal with your anger. It is my greatest regret. Please forgive me. I love you.

CHAPTER 67

Anna's Miracle-My Father's Ancestry

Linda: A woman named Anna Schierse contacted me a year after Keith died.

She had found her last name on a book at a Slavic friend's house. This was a Slavic translation of *The Wounded Woman*. Wondering if we might be relatives, Anna read two of my books and called the *Los Angeles Jung Institute* for my address.

What a gift! Now I had a living relative. We agreed to meet in Berlin where she worked for the German Film Archive. She loved film as much as me! With her help, I also met another cousin, Katerina, who was a psychiatrist working in Trier. Remarkably, Katerina was a living part of my Schierse family history, too.

Anna and I decided to go to Silesia (a place that changed nationality back and forth between Poland and Germany) to explore family history.

We learned that my grandfather was the oldest of sixteen children. Anna's great-granduncle was a brother to my grandfather and they had worked together in the bakery and wine business before my grandfather emigrated to Philadelphia in 1890.

Surprisingly, many of these Schierse brothers were scientists, doctors, and the youngest was a musician who started a music school, similar to Juilliard, for young musicians in Berlin.

I had heard only bad things about my grandfather—that he was an alcoholic who knocked over a stove that started a fire during a drunken debauch. He forced my father to quit school at the age of twelve, stiflingly his great desire to get an education.

Secretly I had always wondered if I was related to a gang of criminals. Now I learned that the thirst for knowledge and love of music was in my father's blood!

Anna and I went to Breslau where our relatives had lived. We tracked down the address of our ancestral home and learned it had been bombed by Americans during World War II. We two paid homage to this site and then found a place in the countryside where we believed my grandfather had been conceived. Anna located the address of her great-granduncle's family home and prayed for him there.

Together we loved Breslau, known for its Market Square, lined with elegant townhouses and featuring a modern fountain. The old town was lovely and we ate many Polish dumplings. Enthused, Anna, who had a talent for languages, decided to learn Polish. She already spoke and wrote in excellent English.

So started a wonderful relationship between Anna, a living relative I never knew I had. Celebrating back in Berlin, we went to see Sir Simon Rattle, a British conductor with German citizenship who rose to international prominence, as well as to the opera, *Tristan and Isolde*, conducted by Daniel Barenboim. We enjoyed some rare films in the theatre of the German Film Archive where Anna worked.

So, Dad, starting in 2017, I had a first chance to get to know your heritage better.

I wrote *The Wounded Woman* to reconcile with you. Now I had living evidence through Anna that you came from a family that valued education. It helped explain why I was so different from my mother.

Today, some eight years later, Anna and I email each other nearly every week. And all this because my book happened to be translated in Slavic and my wonderful cousin, Anna, saw it and found me.

Thank you, Dad, for your wonderful heritage, and for your name, Schierse, which brought Anna into my life.

Linda by the fountain in the Cathedral of Santiago de Compostela.

CHAPTER 68

Walking The Way of Saint James

Linda's Letter to Keith:

Dear Sweetheart,

Today I started walking the *Camino de Santiago de Compostela*, the ancient pilgrimage to the holy site, the shrine of Saint James, in Spain. You and I had talked about the Camino many times since we are both journeyers and have made many pilgrimages together. Walking a sacred way together is one of the things I love most about you. I love that you aim to lead a spiritual life and that you share that with me. I also love that you hiked and ran and that, for me, every footstep leaves a sacred mark on the earth.

At seventy I am walking the Camino for both of us since you are eighty-four and your legs are worn out. So my two legs are really four (your two and my two) and I hope I have enough stamina at my age to walk it carrying you within me.

Our good friend and colleague, Terry Gibson, asked me to co-lead a small group for this event. Also on the trip is Hilary Cadwell, a special friend, a favorite because of her openness and spirit. She is a psychologist, an authentic movement body worker, and worked with outpatient psychotics from the Mission district. Every morning Terry leads a ritual to enter the sacred space that is the Camino. And of course we begin with prayer, and so, Keith, you are in that prayer, too. And then we walk in silence until the end of the day.

As you know *Santiago de Compostela* means "St. James of the Field of Stars," because it is believed that the remains of the Apostle St. James the Great rest in the great cathedral there. The stars in the night sky form the Milky Way which guides the pilgrim. And you, Keith, are a lover of stars, and led our trips in the Southwest to see the stars through the best telescopes. So walking this Camino of the "Field of Stars" fits perfectly for you. Together in my heart, we will be guided by the Milky Way!

In the Middle Ages there were many Camino routes to the cathedral because pilgrims would start from their homes and their trails would intersect. As you are a lover of history, I am sure you are reading and studying this lore now and following me as you read. I love that you are a Renaissance man and follow your passions with study. We are both students of life.

People of all ages and cultures walk the Camino. An older woman from Hungary, who had hurt her leg coming from the Pyrenees, greeted us. She had the determined spirit that would help make her goal. You, who admire survivors, would have loved talking to her.

You would also love the farmers who greeted us with "*Buen Camino!*" as we passed through their beautiful farms. They are a very special part of the way. And if a person fell ill or was injured, they were given free care in hospitals in Spain. And in my Camino dream, you, Dr. Keith, would have been at the hospitals helping to care for the injured. You were so faithful to your Hippocratic Oath. I loved this about you—your dedication to healing.

Every afternoon we would gather to talk about the events of our day. Hilary and I sat together. One man started talking but he couldn't stop. The rest of us didn't know what to do. He just went on and on. Suddenly we heard strange sounds and movement—grunting and groaning and whistling. It was Hilary who was also shaking her body! The talking man even stopped to look. Hilary, a movement teacher and therapist, spontaneously did what it took to break through the group's hurdle with the talking man. And we were thankful. Hilary added laughter to our group.

Keith, the last day of my trek, when we would reach the Cathedral of Compostela, I said this as my morning prayer to you.

"Keith, you and I didn't talk that much. We shared silence. We shared interests and activities. You understood me and that might be the most important thing. Also we shared values. And we shared feelings. We shared dreams. And we were not like a normal couple. We were not domestic. I wanted to see the world. And you, too—I could travel to the ends of the earth with you! You and I lived fully in our professions. We were in a deep Jungian analysis, which is what brought us together. And we were mystics; we wanted that deep soul relationship. And through our struggles, I found that soulmate relationship with you. Thank you. You have my love."

Keith, the last day to Santiago was grueling. Pilgrims had to walk miles through the city before reaching the Cathedral. Once there, we knelt in prayer to St. James and all those who had come here before, and we attended the Pilgrim's Mass held each day. Before entering the Cathedral, we touched a pillar now worn down and marked by the hands of devotion, touched as well the Scallop sea shell symbolic of the pilgrimage, and prayed with gratitude to the Divinity in Heaven that we were given the grace to complete the journey. We received the Pilgrim's Pass, a certificate of accomplishment, that showed completion of the footpath under the stars of the Milky Way.

While the pilgrimage demanded pain and suffering, each sacred step, with you within me, left its imprint on earth, marking our souls' journey, and our I-Thou relationship, on our path together with all of humanity and with the Divine.

Love,

Linda

Hope to see you soon.

The Firebird falls.

CHAPTER 69

The Firebird

"Once upon a time there was an orphan girl, Maryushka, who could embroider more beautifully than anyone else in the land. Although she was gentle, modest, and quiet, her fame spread over the land and across the seas to merchants who came to see her wonderful work and offer her riches if she would come to work for them. But Maryushka always declined for she wanted to stay in the village where she was born. And so the merchants left singing her praises wherever they went. One day the sorcerer, Koschei the Immortal, heard of Maryushka's fabrics and it angered him to learn there was a beauty in the world that did not belong to him.

"Changing his form to a handsome young man, he flew far away, across the great steppes of Russia to Maryushka's Russian home. As was the custom, when he met Maryushka, he bowed low to her and asked to see her embroidery. Whereupon she took out her fine needlework and offered it to him to see. The sight of so much beauty that a simple country girl could create, and that he himself did not possess, drove Koschei into a frenzy. So, with a cunning tone, he proposed to Maryushka and asked her to be his queen. She could live in a palace of jewels, eat off plates of gold, sleep on eiderdown, and enjoy the golden apples and birds of paradise singing in his orchards. But Maryushka refused his offer—she would not embroider for him alone. She loved the green pastures and woods and the village where she was born, where the townsfolk found joy in her work.

"When Koschei heard her answer, he was furious. Instantly he changed her into a beautiful firebird. He himself became a great black falcon and swooped upon the lovely firebird, grasping her in his talons and flying off with her into the sky. But Maryushka resolved to sacrifice her life in order to leave her beauty for others on the earth. So she shed her brilliant rainbow colored feathers, which one by one floated to the ground. And now these feathers of the firebird shine with magic as gifts for all those on earth who love beauty and seek to create it for others."

—With thanks, this is based upon the retelling of the Firebird story by Suzanne Massie

Jean Le Fou: Linda, thanks for writing. This story of Maryushka and the Firebird—it's vivid and true to me. Can I ask you a very personal question? Since we're friends. I know you. And you know me.

Maryushka is you in this story. The wonderful person, on her own, creating her beauty, being seen, understood, admired. You having created great works of your art, admired across our homeland.

But who in this story is Koschei, the evil sorcerer, who would keep you prisoner, steal your beauty? Is this your father who burned down your home, killed one of your family, stole your childhood?

Or is Koschei your mother, who could not let you go? Who kept you prisoner, who, even as you left for a new life, had a car accident that might have kept you from leaving? Wanting you with her forever, in spite of whatever of your beauties had to be sacrificed?

I can see that Koschei could be either one of these two people. Both placed huge burdens—emotional burdens, social burdens, spiritual burdens—on you at childhood. That somehow you lived through. When most would be lost.

I know you rose, a Firebird, dropping feathers of beauty behind, to leave the horribleness of that world, and find your own.

But who, dear Linda, was Koschei in this story?

❤️ 🙏

Jean

Linda: Hello, Jean. Koschei is an archetypal figure—the Demon Lover—but he gets lived out through real-life figures. And perhaps with my mother and father at certain times, and definitely in addiction… Or other ways we choose a destructive way instead of a creative path. I used the Firebird story to end my book on addiction.

I did not see Maryushka as me, but it is wonderful that you do.

Epilogue Healing Keith at Home

Keith (running into my room, panicked): I'm going to die! I'm going to die! Linda help me. I know I'm going to die!

Linda: Sweetheart, calm down. Sit beside me. Take my hand. Tell me what is upsetting you so.

Keith: I feel it. I know I'm going to die and I'm afraid.

Linda: I know what will help.

Come into the living room and sit on the couch. We can do a ritual for healing together. I'll set up our small round Indian coffee table and bring our Russian reindeer bowls and you should bring your children's photos while I bring a picture of you and me. Now look. I am pouring milk into the colorful bowl—the one we bought from Russian children on the roadside. The milk is reindeer milk used for healing by the reindeer people in Siberia. We will pray and drink the milk together and honor life and the Reindeer Goddess in this way. Then you will feel better, I promise.

There. We are drinking the milk and thanking the reindeer, and praying in gratitude for the beauty of the bowl, the holy cup, and the divinity of our hearts.

Now I can see that you feel better. You are not alone. We are wedded together as soulmates in a vow to love each other and our devotion to the divine spirit of all life.

Keith Chapman, MD.

Beloved Psychiatrist who helped all in need
Sept. 16, 1923 – March, 6, 2016
Atlanta, Georgia   Boulder, Colorado

Beloved Soulmate and Healer of the Heart
Healer of the poor, ill, and injured
Healer of the Wounded
Healer of the Mad and Crazy

"Love all God's creation, the whole and every grain of sand in it. Love every leaf, every ray of God's light. Love the animals, love the plants, love everything. If you love everything, you will perceive the divine mystery in things."

Dostoyevsky
The Brothers Karamazov

About The Authors

Linda Schierse Leonard, Ph.D., is the bestselling author of *The Wounded Woman* now translated in 20 languages. She is also author of the best sellers *On the Way to the Wedding*, *Witness to the Fire*, *Meeting the Madwoman*, also translated in other languages, and *Following the Reindeer Woman* and *The Call to Create*. She is a Jungian analyst trained in Zurich, a founding member of *The Inter-Regional Society of Jungian Analysts*, an international lecturer, and a philosopher who taught at San Diego State University and University of Colorado, Denver. Currently she is based in San Francisco.

Bill G. Morris is a San Francisco writer who has published six computer and educational books, written as a software columnist for the *San Francisco Chronicle,* and published five books of essays and ten works of fiction, including *Conversations with Death,* his most recent book, co-authored with Dr. Pamela Eakins. He first read Linda Schierse Leonard's *The Wounded Woman* at thirty-five and his life changed. Forty-years later he wrote a letter of thanks to Linda for her work, and as miracles would have it, they became friends and wrote *Keith's Book* together, he as the voice of *Keith*, *Jean Le Fou,* and *Snooks the Horse*. A wonderful journey.

Made in United States
Orlando, FL
16 September 2026

87759402R00164